Anecdotes & Stories of

ABRAHAM
LINCOLN

0 11557 03346 5

THE 16TH PRESIDENT OF THE UNITED STATES

Anecdotes & Stories of

ABRAHAM LINCOLN

EARLY LIFE STORIES

PROFESSIONAL LIFE STORIES

WHITE HOUSE STORIES

WAR STORIES

MISCELLANEOUS STORIES

Edited by J. B. McClure

STACKPOLE
BOOKS

A Stackpole Classic Reprint, 2006

Stackpole Books
5067 Ritter Road
Mechanicsburg, PA 17055-6921
www.stackpolebooks.com

Originally published in 1888 by Rhodes & McClure Publishing Co.,
    Chicago

Cover design by Wendy Reynolds

Printed in the United States of America

10 9 8 7 6 5 4 3 2 1

Library of Congress Cataloging-in-Publication Data

Lincoln, Abraham, 1809–1865.
  [Anecdotes of Abraham Lincoln and Lincoln's stories]
  Anecdotes and stories of Abraham Lincoln : early life stories,
professional life stories, White House stories, war stories, miscellaneous
stories / edited by J. B. McClure.
      p. cm. — (A Stackpole classic reprint)
  "Originally published in 1884 by Rhodes & McClure Publishing Co.,
Chicago."
  Includes index.
  ISBN 0-8117-3346-7 (pbk. : alk. paper)
  1. Lincoln, Abraham, 1809–1865—Anecdotes. I. McClure, J. B. (James
Baird), 1832–1895. II. Title. III. Series.

E457.99.M12 2006
973.7092—dc22

2006011299

ISBN 978-0-8117-3346-5

PREFACE

SAID Mr. Lincoln, to Dr. Gulliver, on a certain occasion when the versatile Doctor had highly complimented the then coming President concerning one of his speeches:

" I should very much like to know what it was in my speech which you thought so remarkable, and which interested my friend, the Professor (of Yale College), so much ? "

" The clearness," answered Dr. G., " of your statements, the unanswerable style of your reasoning and especially your *illustrations, which were romance, and pathos, and fun, and logic, all welded together.*"

The great Lincoln thanked the clerical celebrity, and said: "That reminds me of a story," and then proceeded to tell how the Yale Professor had taken notes on his New Haven speech, and had lectured his class, and had followed him to Meriden for further " notes," etc.

Thus is demonstrated the superior value that attaches to Mr. Lincoln's "illustrations," which, as all the world knows, were made of pointed, pungent, pithy and practical *stories*, drawn from an inexhaustible source, and always available on every possible occasion. Perhaps there never lived a greater story-teller than Abraham Lincoln, and one who told them always with such magic effect. With him, the "appropriate story " was a *power*, and his remarkable faculty in telling them was an essential factor in his greatness.

In this volume the compiler has aimed to present, in a conveniently classified form, the Anecdotes and Stories of this wonderful man, as narrated by him to the lowly and the great, in peace and war, at the fireside and bar, in the wilderness and White-house, with that zest and potency which made Mr. Lincoln such a remarkable man. It is our sincere desire that in this form the book may be of real interest and prove a further means of *usefulness* to every reader.

Our indebtedness is specially acknowledged for aid found in F. B. Carpenter's "Six Months in the White-house;" J. G. Holland's "Life of Lincoln;" the Press, and to the many friends who have contributed.

J. B. McCLURE.

CHICAGO, ILL., January 1, 1888.

CONTENTS

EARLY LIFE.

A Batch of Lincoln's Reminiscences 49

A Hard Tussle with Seven Negroes—Life on a Mississippi Flat Boat 27

A Humorous Speech—Lincoln in the Black Hawk War 39

A Pig Story—Lincoln's Kindness to the Brute Creation 26

An Honest Boy—Young Lincoln "Pulls Fodder" Two Days for a Damaged Book 14

An Incident of Lincoln's Early Hardships 18

An Incident or Two Illustrating Lincoln's Honesty 22

Captain Lincoln—How he Became Captain 38

Elected to the Legislature—Lincoln Walks to the State Capitol ... 41

General Linder's Early Recollections of Lincoln 46

How Lincoln Earned his First Dollar 13

How Lincoln Helped to Build a Boat—How he Loaded the Live Stock 23

How Lincoln Piloted a Flat Boat over a Mill Dam 34

Lincoln and his Gentle Annie—A Touching Incident 20

Lincoln's First Political Speech 40

Lincoln's Marriage—Some very Interesting Letters 44

Lincoln's Mechanical Ingenuity—His Patent Boat 31

Lincoln's Mother—How he Loved Her 45

Lincoln Splits Several Hundred Rails for a Pair of Pants 28

Lincoln's Story of a Girl in New Salem 29

Little Lincoln Firing at Big Game Through the Cracks of his Cabin Home 17

Mrs. Brown's Story of Young Abe 30

Remarkable Story—"Honest Abe" as Postmaster 32

Returning from the Legislature—A Joke on Lincoln's Big Feet .. 43

Showing How Lincoln Resented an Insult 24

6

CONTENTS. 7

Splitting Rails and Studying Mathematics 84
"The Long Nine"—Lincoln the Longest of All 42
What some Men say About Young Lincoln 25
When and Where Lincoln Obtained the Name of "Honest Abe," 31
Young Lincoln and his Books—Their Influence on his Mind 19
Young Lincoln and the "Clary's Grove Boys," 48
Young Lincoln's Kindness of Heart 18

PROFESSIONAL LIFE.

A Famous Story—How Lincoln was Presented with a Knife 60
A Revolutionary Prisoner Defended by Lincoln 75
An Amusing Story concerning Thompson Campbell 60
An Honest Lawyer—Some of Lincoln's Cases 74
An Incident Related by one of Lincoln's Clients 64
General Linder's Account of the Lincoln-Shields Duel 71
How Lincoln and Judge B—— Swapped Horses 55
How Lincoln kept his Business Accounts 68
Honest Abe and his Lady Client 67
Hon. Newton Bateman's Story of Mr. Lincoln 79
Incident Connected with Lincoln's Nomination 70
Lincoln and "His Sisters and his Cousins, and his Aunts," 67
Lincoln and his Step-mother—How he Bought her a Farm 59
Lincoln as a Story Teller—A Practical Example 77
Lincoln Defends the Son of an Old Friend Indicted for Murder .. 72
Lincoln in Court 68
Lincoln's Pungent Retort 74
Lincoln's Story of a Young Lawyer as told to General Garfield .. 58
Lincoln's Story of Joe Wilson and his "Spotted Animals," 63
Lincoln's Valor—He Defends Col. Baker 65
One of Lincoln's Hardest Hits 69
Remarkable Law Suit about a Colt—How Lincoln Won the Case, 55
The Lincoln-Shields Duel—How it Originated 16
Thrilling Story—Lincoln's Twenty Years' Agitation in Illinois ... 76

WHITE HOUSE INCIDENTS.

A Home Incident—Lincoln and Little "Tad," 105
A Little Story which Lincoln told the Preachers 85
A Praying President—"Prayer and Praise," 120
A "Pretty Tolerable Respectable Sort of a Clergyman," 94
An Apt Illustration 90

8 *CONTENTS.*

An Instance where the President's Mind Wandered............... 104
An Irish Soldier who wanted Something Stronger than Soda
  Water.. 90
Comments of Mr. Lincoln on the Emancipation Proclamation.... 109
Common Sense.. 93
Criticism—Its Effect on Mr. Lincoln—A Bull Frog Story......... 111
Ejecting a Cashiered Officer from the White House................. 113
How Lincoln and Stanton Dismissed Applicants for Office....... 101
How Lincoln " Browsed Around,".................................... 100
How Lincoln Opened the Eyes of a Visitor......................... 97
How Lincoln Stood up for the Word "Sugar Coated,"............. 86
How the Negroes Regarded "Massa Linkum,".................... 115
Lincoln's Advice to a Prominent Bachelor......................... 87
Lincoln and the Committee on "Grant's Whisky,"............... 94
Lincoln and the Newspapers.. 111
Lincoln and the Preacher... 104
Lincoln and the Wall Street Gold Gamblers....................... 114
Lincoln Arguing Against the Emancipation Proclamation....... 110
Lincoln Cutting Red Tape... 100
Lincoln's Habits in the White House—The Same "Old Abe,".... 117
Lincoln's High Compliment to the Women of America........... 118
Lincoln in the Hour of Deep Sorrow—He Recalls his Mother's
  Prayers.. 118
Lincoln's Laugh.. 111
Lincoln's Little Speech to the Union League Committee.... 113
Lincoln Mourning for his Lost Son is Comforted by Rev. Dr. Vinton, 106
Looking out for Breakers.. 91
Lincoln's Story of a Poodle Dog...................................... 112
Lincoln Wipes the Tears from his Eyes, and Tells a Story........ 109
Minnehaha and Minneboohoo.. 97
More Light and Less Noise... 99
Mr. Lincoln and the Bashful Boys.................................... 88
One of Lincoln's Drolleries 101
One of Lincoln's Last Stories.. 116
President Lincoln and the Artist, Carpenter....................... 97
Telling a Story and Pardoning a Soldier—Lincoln did Both....... 121
The Kind of Cane Lincoln Made and Carried when a Boy....... 92
Trying the "Greens" on Jake—A Serious Experiment........... 85
Stories Illustrating Lincoln's Memory............................... 92
Work Enough for Twenty Presidents................................. 91

WAR STORIES.

A Celebrated Case Settled with Lincoln-like Celerity............ 140
A Church which God Wanted for the Wounded Soldiers.......... 144
A Dream that was Portentous—What Lincoln Said to General Grant About it... 147
A Little Soldier Boy that Lincoln wanted to Bow to............. 127
Amusing Anecdote of a "Hen-pecked Husband,"............... 138
A Short Practical Sermon.................................... 139
A Soldier that Knew no Royalty.............................. 126
A Touching Incident in the Life of Lincoln................... 132
An Interesting Visit to the Hospitals—How the Soldiers Received Him 132
Could not allow a Soldier to be more Polite than Himself........ 131
Cutting Reply to the Confederate Commission—His Story of "Root Hog or Die,".. 155
How Lincoln Illustrated What Might Be Done with Jeff Davis.. 154
How Lincoln Relieved Rosecrans............................. 145
Interesting Incident Connected with Signing the Emancipation Proclamation 146
Lincoln and Judge Baldwin................................. 148
Lincoln's Curt Reply to a Clergyman......................... 139
Lincoln Proposes to "Borrow the Army" from one of his Generals 131
Lincoln's Second Nomination—Lincoln Sees Two Images of himself in a Mirror... 153
Lincoln's War Story of Andy Johnson—Col. Moody's Prayers.... 125
Lincoln While in Bed Pardons a Soldier...................... 128
Mr. Lincoln and a Clergyman............................... 134
No Mercy for the Man Stealer—Lincoln Uses Very Strong Language 151
Recollections of the War President, by Judge William Johnson.. 141
Remarkable Letter from Lincoln to General Hooker............. 135
Sallie Ward's Practical Philosophy........................... 128
The Great Thing About General Grant as Lincoln Saw it........ 153
The Merciful President..................................... 150
The Serpent in Bed with Two Children....................... 143
What Lincoln Considered the "Great Event of the Nineteenth Century "... 130

10 CONTENTS.

MISCELLANEOUS STORIES.

A couple of good Stories—How Lincoln took his Altitude—A Prophetic Bowl of Milk 169
Abraham Lincoln's Death—Walt Whitman's description of the Scene at Ford's Theatre 184
An Amusing Illustration 168
Attending Henry Ward Beecher's Church—What Lincoln said of Beecher 159
D. L. Moody's Story of Lincoln's Compassion 176
Feat at the Washington Navy Yard with an Axe 162
Funeral Services of Lincoln's Mother—The Old Pastor and Young Abraham 164
How Lincoln Won a Case from his Partner—Laughable Toilet Ignorance 179
Interesting Anecdote of Lincoln related by Rev. J. P. Gulliver... 173
Lincoln and his New Hat 162
Lincoln and the Little Baby—A Touching Story 175
Lincoln at the Five Points House of Industry at New York 161
Lincoln's Failure as a Merchant—Six Years later he pays his Debts 163
Lincoln Joking Douglas—A Splendid "Whisky Cask," 178
Lincoln's Last Story and Last Written Words and Conversations. 182
Lincoln's Life as written by himself—The whole thing in a Nutshell 179
Lincoln's Love for Little Tad 160
Lincoln's Love for the Little Ones 170
Lincoln's Story about Dan Webster's Soiled Hands 175
Little Lincoln Stories 180
Something concerning Mr. Lincoln's Religious Views 166
Thurlow Weed's Recollections 167

ILLUSTRATIONS

ABRAHAM LINCOLN, Sixteenth President of the U. S.......Frontispiece
UNITED STATES CAPITOL......................Vignette, Title Page
EARLY HOME OF THE LINCOLNS IN ILLINOIS...................... 36
BIRTH PLACE OF ABRAHAM LINCOLN............................. 16
ILLINOIS STATE CAPITOL, SPRINGFIELD, ILLINOIS.............. 54
ABRAHAM LINCOLN, the LAWYER............................... 66
UNITED STATES CAPITOL AT WASHINGTON...................... 84
WHITE PIGEON CHURCH....................................... 96
LINCOLN MONUMENT, SPRINGFIELD, ILLINOIS.................... 124
DOUGLAS MONUMENT, CHICAGO................. 138
HOME OF THE LINCOLNS IN INDIANA........................... 158
ABRAHAM LINCOLN'S RESIDENCE AT SPRINGFIELD, ILLINOIS..... 172

CLASSIFICATIONS

EARLY LIFE STORIES.. 13
PROFESSIONAL LIFE STORIES................................. 55
WHITE-HOUSE INCIDENTS..................................... 85
WAR STORIES.. 125
MISCELLANEOUS STORIES.................................... 159

ANECDOTES

OF

ABRAHAM LINCOLN.

EARLY LIFE.

How Lincoln Earned His First Dollar.

The following interesting story was told by Mr. Lincoln to Mr. Seward and a few friends one evening in the Executive Mansion at Washington. The President said : "Seward, you never heard, did you, how I earned my first dollar ?" "No," rejoined Mr. Seward. "Well," continued Mr. Lincoln, "I belonged, you know, to what they call down South, the 'scrubs.' We had succeeded in raising, chiefly by my labor, sufficient produce, as I thought, to justify me in taking it down the river to sell.

"After much persuasion, I got the consent of mother to go, and constructed a little flatboat, large enough to take a barrel or two of things that we had gathered, with myself and little bundle, down to the Southern market. A steamer was coming down the river. We have, you know, no wharves on the Western streams ; and the custom was, if passengers were at any of the landings, for them to go out in a boat, the steamer stopping and taking them on board.

"I was contemplating my new flatboat, and wondering whether I could make it stronger or improve it in any par-

ticular, when two men came down to the shore in carriages
with trunks, and looking at the different boats singled out
mine, and asked, 'Who owns this?'   I answered, somewhat
modestly, 'I do.' 'Will you,' said one of them, 'take us
and our trunks out to the steamer?' 'Certainly,' said I.
I was very glad to have the chance of earning something.
I supposed that each of them would give me two or three
bits.   The trunks were put on my flatboat, the passengers
seated themselves on the trunks, and I sculled them out to
the steamboat.

"They got on board, and I lifted up their heavy trunks,
and put them on deck. The steamer was about to put on
steam again, when I called out that they had forgotten to
pay me. Each of them took from his pocket a silver half-
dollar, and threw it on the floor of my boat. I could
scarcely believe my eyes as I picked up the money. Gentlemen, you may think it was a very little thing, and in these
days it seems to me a trifle ; but it was a most important
incident in my life. I could scarcely credit that I, a poor
boy, had earned a dollar in less than a day—that by honest
work I had earned a dollar   The world seemed wider and
fairer before me. I was a more hopeful and confident being
from that time."

**An Honest Boy—Young Lincoln "Pulls Fodder" Two Days for
a Damaged Book.**

The following incident, illustrating several traits already
developed in the early boyhood of Lincoln, is vouched for
by a citizen of Evansville, Ind., who knew him in the days
referred to :

In his eagerness to acquire knowledge, young Lincoln
had borrowed of Mr. Crawford, a neighboring farmer, a
copy of Weems' Life of Washington—the only one known

BIRTH-PLACE OF ABRAHAM LINCOLN.

In what is now LaRue Co., Kentucky, one and a half miles from Hodgenville, and seven miles from Elizabethtown. The three pear trees were planted by Lincoln's father, and mark the spot near where the house stood. Abraham Lincoln was born February 12, 1809. He resided here only a few years.

to be in existence in that region of country. Before he had finished reading the book, it had been left, by a not unnatural oversight, in a window. Meantime, a rain storm came on, and the book was so thoroughly wet as to make it nearly worthless. This mishap caused him much pain ; but he went, in all honesty, to Mr. Crawford with the ruined book, explained the calamity that had happened through his neglect, and offered, not having sufficient money, to " work out " the value of the book.

" Well, Abe," said Mr. Crawford, after due deliberation, " as it's you, I won't be hard on you. Just come over and pull fodder for me for two days, and we will call our accounts even."

The offer was readily accepted, and the engagement literally fulfilled. As a boy, no less than since, Abraham Lincoln had an honorable conscientiousness, integrity, industry, and an ardent love of knowledge.

Little Lincoln Firing at Big Game Through the Cracks of His Cabin Home.

While yet a little boy, one day when Lincoln was in his cabin home, in what was then a wilderness in Indiana, he chanced to look through a crack in the log walls of the humble residence and espied a flock of wild turkeys feeding within range of his father's trusty rifle. He at once took in the possibilities of the situation and ventured to take down the old gun, and quietly putting the long barrel through the opening, with a hasty aim, fired into the flock. When the smoke had cleared away, it was observed that one of the turkeys lay dead on the field. This is said to have been the largest game on which Lincoln ever pulled a trigger, his brilliant success in this instance having no power to excite in him the passion for hunting.

An Incident of Lincoln's Early Hardships and Narrow Escape from Death.

A little incident occurred while young Lincoln lived in Indiana, which illustrates the early hardships and surround-ings to which he was subjected. On one occasion he was obliged to take his grist upon the back of his father's horse, and go *fifty miles* to get it ground. The mill itself was very rude, and driven by horse-power. The customers were obliged to wait their " turn," without reference to their distance from home, and then use their own horse to propel the machinery ! On this occasion, Abraham, having arrived at his turn, fastened his mare to the lever, and was following her closely upon her rounds, when, urging her with a switch, and "clucking" to her in the usual way, he received a kick from her which prostrated him, and made him insensible. With the first instant of returning con-sciousness, he finished the cluck, which he had commenced when he received the kick (a fact for the psychologist), and with the next he probably thought about getting home, where he arrived at last, battered, but ready for further service.

Young Lincoln's Kindness of Heart—He Carries Home and Nurses a Drunkard.

An instance of young Lincoln's practical humanity at an early period of his life is recorded, as follows : One even-ing, while returning from a " raising " in his wide neigh-borhood, with a number of companions, he discovered a straying horse, with saddle and bridle upon him. The horse was recognized as belonging to a man who was accus-tomed to excess in drink, and it was suspected at once that the owner was not far off. A short search only was neces-sary to confirm the suspicions of the young men.

The poor drunkard was found in a perfectly helpless condition, upon the chilly ground. Abraham's companions urged the cowardly policy of leaving him to his fate, but young Lincoln would not hear to the proposition. At his request, the miserable sot was lifted to his shoulders, and he actually carried him eighty rods to the nearest house. Sending word to his father that he should not be back that night, with the reason for his absence, he attended and nursed the man until the morning, and had the pleasure of believing that he had saved his life.

Young Lincoln and His Books—Their Influence on His Mind.

The books which Abraham had the early privilege of reading were the Bible, much of which he could repeat, Æsop's Fables, all of which he could repeat, Pilgrim's Progress, Weems' Life of Washington, and a Life of Henry Clay, which his mother had managed to purchase for him. Subsequently he read the Life of Franklin and Ramsey's Life of Washington. In these books, read and re-read, he found meat for his hungry mind. The Holy Bible, Æsop and John Bunyan—could three better books have been chosen for him from the richest library?

For those who have witnessed the dissipating effects of many books upon the minds of modern children it is not hard to believe that Abraham's poverty of books was the wealth of his life. These three books did much to perfect that which his mother's teachings had begun, and to form a character which, for quaint simplicity, earnestness, truthfulness and purity has never been surpassed among the historic personages of the world. The Life of Washington, while it gave to him a lofty example of patriotism, incidentally conveyed to his mind a general knowledge of American history; and the Life of Henry Clay spoke to him of a living man who had risen to political and professional eminence from circumstances almost as humble as his own.

The latter book undoubtedly did much to excite his taste for politics, to kindle his ambition, and to make him a warm admirer and partisan of Henry Clay. Abraham must have been very young when he read Weems' Life of Washington, and we catch a glimpse of his precocity in the thoughts which it excited, as revealed by himself in a speech made to the New Jersey Senate, while on his way to Washington to assume the duties of the Presidency.

Alluding to his early reading of this book, he says: " I remember all the accounts there given of the battle fields and struggles for the liberties of the country, and none fixed themselves upon my imagination so deeply as the struggle here at Trenton, New Jersey. * * * *I recollect thinking then, boy even though I was, that there must have been something more than common that those men struggled for.*" Even at this age, he was not only an interested reader of the story, but a student of motives.

Lincoln and His Gentle Annie—A Touching Incident.

The following interesting particulars connected with the early life of Abraham Lincoln, are from the Virginia (Ill.) *Enquirer*, of date March 1, 1879:

John McNamer was buried last Sunday, near Petersburg, Menard County. A long while ago he was Assessor and Treasurer of the county for several successive terms. Mr. McNamer was an early settler in that section, and before the Town of Petersburg was laid out was in business at Old Salem, a village that existed many years ago two miles south of the present site of Petersburg. Abe Lincoln was then postmaster of the place, and sold whisky to its inhabitants. There are old-timers yet living in Menard who bought many a jug of corn-juice from Old Abe when he lived at Salem. It was here that Annie Rutlege dwelt, and in whose grave Lincoln wrote that his heart was buried. As the story runs, the fair and gentle Annie was originally John McNamer's sweetheart, but Abe took a " shine " to the young lady, and succeeded in heading off McNamer, and won her affections. But Annie Rutlege died, and Lincoln went to Springfield, where he some time afterwards married.

It is related that during the war a lady belonging to a prominent Kentucky family visited Washington to beg for her son's pardon, who was then in prison under sentence of death for belonging to a band of guerrillas who had committed many murders and outrages. With the mother was her daughter, a beautiful young lady, who was an accomplished musician. Mr. Lincoln received the visitors in his usual kind manner, and the mother made known the object of her visit, accompanying her plea with tears and sobs and all the customary dramatic incidents.

There were probably extenuating circumstances in favor of the young Rebel prisoner, and while the President seemed to be deeply pondering, the young lady moved to a piano near by, and taking a seat commenced to sing " Gentle Annie," a very sweet and pathetic ballad, which, before the war, was a familiar song in almost every household in the Union, and is not yet entirely forgotten, for that matter. It is to be presumed the young lady sang the song with more plaintiveness and effect than Old Abe had ever heard it in Springfield. During its rendition, he arose from his seat, crossed the room to a window in the westward, through which he gazed for several minutes with that " sad, far-away look," which has so often been noted as one of his peculiarities. His memory, no doubt, went back to the days of his humble life on the banks of the Sangamon, and with visions of Old Salem and its rustic people, who once gathered in his primitive store, came a picture of the " Gentle Annie " of his youth, whose ashes had rested for many long years under the wild flowers and brambles of the old rural burying-ground, but whose spirit then, perhaps, guided him to the side of mercy. Be that as it may, Mr. Lincoln drew a large red silk handkerchief from his coat-pocket, with which he wiped his face vigorously. Then he turned, advanced quickly to his desk, wrote a brief note, which he handed to the lady, and informed her that it was the pardon she sought.

The scene was no doubt touching in a great degree, and proves that a nice song, well sung, has often a powerful influence in recalling tender recollections. It proves, also, that Abraham Lincoln was a man of fine feelings, and that, if the occurrence was a put-up job on the lady's part, it accomplished its purpose all the same.

An Incident or Two Illustrating Lincoln's Honesty.

Lincoln could not rest for an instant under the consciousness that he had, even unwittingly, defrauded anybody. On one occasion, while clerking in Offutt's store, at New Salem, Ill., he sold a woman a little bill of goods, amounting in value by the reckoning, to two dollars six and a quarter cents. He received the money, and the woman went away. On adding the items of the bill again, to make himself sure of correctness, he found that he had taken six and a quarter cents too much. It was night, and, closing and locking the store, he started out on foot, a distance of two or three miles, for the house of his defrauded customer, and, delivering over to her the sum whose possession had so much troubled him, went home satisfied.

On another occasion, just as he was closing the store for

the night, a woman entered, and asked for a half pound of tea. The tea was weighed out and paid for, and the store was left for the night. The next morning, Lincoln entered to begin the duties of the day, when he discovered a four-ounce weight on the scales. He saw at once that he had made a mistake, and, shutting the store, he took a long walk before breakfast to deliver the remainder of the tea. These are very humble incidents, but they illustrate the man's perfect conscientiousness—his sensitive honesty—better perhaps than they would if they were of greater moment.

How Lincoln Helped to Build a Boat, and How He Loaded the Live Stock.

While a laboring man, Lincoln, Hanks & Johnston on one occasion contracted to build a boat on Sangamon River, at Sangamon Town, about seven miles northwest of Springfield. For this work they were to receive twelve dollars a month each. When the boat was finished (and every plank of it was sawed by hand with a whip-saw), it was launched on the Sangamon, and floated to a point below New Salem, in Menard (then Sangamon) County, where a drove of hogs was to be taken on board. At this time, the hogs of the region ran wild, as they do now in portions of the border states. Some of them were savage, and all, after the manner of swine, were difficult to manage. They had, however, been gathered and penned, but not an inch could they be made to move toward the boat. All the ordinary resources were exhausted in the attempts to get them on board. There was but one alternative, and this Abraham adopted. He actually carried them on board, one by one. His long arms and great strength enabled him to grasp them as in a vise, and to transfer them rapidly from the shore to the boat. They then took the boat to New Orleans, according to contract.

An Incident Showing How Lincoln Resented an Insult—He Gave the Victim a Thrashing.

While showing goods to two or three women in Offutt's store one day, a bully came in and began to talk in an offensive manner, using much profanity, and evidently wishing to provoke a quarrel. Lincoln leaned over the counter, and begged him, as ladies were present, not to indulge in such talk. The bully retorted that the opportunity had come for which he had long sought, and he would like to see the man who could hinder him from saying anything he might choose to say. Lincoln, still cool, told him that if he would wait until the ladies retired, he would hear what he had to say, and give him any satisfaction he desired.

As soon as the women were gone, the man became furious. Lincoln heard his boasts and his abuse for a time, and finding that he was not to be put off without a fight, said—" Well, if you must be whipped, I suppose I may as well whip you as any other man." This was just what the bully had been seeking, he said, so out of doors they went, and Lincoln made short work with him. He threw him upon the ground, held him there as if he had been a child, and gathering some " smart-weed" which grew upon the spot, rubbed it into his face and eyes, until the fellow bellowed with pain. Lincoln did all this without a particle of anger, and when the job was finished, went immediately for water, washed his victim's face, and did everything he could to alleviate his distress. The upshot of the matter was that the man became his fast and life-long friend, and was a better man from that day. It was impossible then, and it always remained impossible, for Lincoln to cherish resentment or revenge.

What Some Men Say About Young Lincoln—His First Meeting With Richard Yates.

Lincoln was a marked and peculiar young man. People talked about him. His studious habits, his greed for information, his thorough mastery of the difficulties of every new position in which he was placed, his intelligence touching all matters of public concern, his unwearying good nature, his skill in telling a story, his great athletic power, his quaint, odd ways, his uncouth appearance, all tending to bring him in sharp contrast with the dull mediocrity by which he was surrounded. Denton Offutt, his old employer in the store, said, in the extravagance of his admiration, that he knew more than any other man in the United States. The Governor of Indiana, one of Offutt's acquaintances, said, after having a conversation with Lincoln, that the young man "had talent enough in him to make a President." In every circle in which he found himself, whether refined or coarse, he was always the centre of attraction.

William G. Greene says that when he (Greene) was a member of Illinois College, he brought home with him, on a vacation, Richard Yates, afterwards Governor of the state, and some other boys, and, in order to entertain them, took them all up to see Lincoln. He found him in his usual position and at his usual occupation. He was flat on his back, on a cellar door, reading a newspaper. That was the manner in which a President of the United States and a Governor of Illinois became acquainted with one another. Mr. Greene says that Lincoln then could repeat the whole of Burns, and was a devoted student of Shakspeare. So the rough backwoodsman, self-educated, entertained the college boys, and was invited to dine with them on bread and milk. How he managed to upset his bowl of milk is not a matter of history, but the fact that he did so is, as is the further fact that Greene's mother, who loved Lincoln, tried to smooth over the accident and relieve the young man's embarrassment.

A Pig Story—Lincoln's Kindness to the Brute Creation.

An amusing incident occurred in connection with "riding the circuit," which gives a pleasant glimpse into the good lawyer's heart. He was riding by a deep slough, in which, to his exceeding pain, he saw a pig struggling, and with such faint efforts that it was evident that he could not extricate himself from the mud. Mr. Lincoln looked at the pig and the mud which enveloped him, and then looked at some new clothes with which he had but a short time before enveloped himself. Deciding against the claims of the pig, he rode on, but he could not get rid of the vision of the poor brute, and, at last, after riding two miles, he turned back, determined to rescue the animal at the expense of his new clothes. Arrived at the spot, he tied his horse, and coolly went to work to build of old rails a passage to the bottom of the hole. Descending on these rails, he seized the pig and dragged him out, but not without serious damage to the clothes he wore. Washing his hands in the nearest brook, and wiping them on the grass, he mounted his gig and rode along. He then fell to examining the motive that sent him back to the release of the pig. At the first thought it seemed to be pure benevolence, but, at length, he came to the conclusion that it was selfishness, for he certainly went to the pig's relief in order (as he said to the friend to whom he related the incident,) to "take a pain out of his own mind." This is certainly a new view of the nature of sympathy, and one which it will be well for the casuist to examine.

A Hard Tussle with Seven Negroes—Life on a Mississippi Flat Boat.

At the age of nineteen, Abraham made his second essay in navigation, and this time caught something more than a glimpse of the great world in which he was destined to play so important a part. A trading neighbor applied to him to take charge of a flat-boat and its cargo, and, in company with his own son, to take it to the sugar plantations near New Orleans. The entire business of the trip was placed in Abraham's hands. The fact tells its own story touching the young man's reputation for capacity and integrity. He had never made the trip, knew nothing of the journey, was unaccustomed to business transactions, had never been much upon the river; but his tact, ability and honesty were so trusted that the trader was willing to risk his cargo and his son in Lincoln's care.

The incidents of a trip like this were not likely to be exciting, but there were many social chats with settlers and hunters along the banks of the Ohio and Mississippi, and there was much hailing of similar craft afloat. Arriving at a sugar plantation somewhere between Natchez and New Orleans, the boat was pulled in, and tied to the shore for purposes of trade; and here an incident occurred which was sufficiently exciting, and one which, in the memory of recent events, reads somewhat strangely. Here seven negroes attacked the life of the future liberator of the race, and it is not improbable that some of them have lived to be emancipated by his proclamation. Night had fallen, and the two tired voyagers had lain down upon their hard bed for sleep. Hearing a noise on shore, Abraham shouted: "Who's there?" The noise continuing, and no voice replying, he sprang to his feet, and saw seven negroes, evidently bent on plunder.

Abraham guessed the errand at once, and seizing a handspike, rushed toward them, and knocked one into the water the moment he touched the boat. The second, third and fourth who leaped on board were served in the same rough way. Seeing that they were not likely to make headway in their thieving enterprise, the remainder turned to flee. Abraham and his companion growing excited and warm with their work, leaped on shore, and followed them. Both were too swift on foot for the negroes, and all of them received a severe pounding. They returned to their boat just as the others escaped from the water, but the latter fled into the darkness as fast as their feet could carry them. Abraham and his fellow in the fight were both injured, but not disabled. Not being armed, and unwilling to wait until the negroes had received reinforcements, they cut adrift, and floating down a mile or two, tied up to the bank again, and watched and waited for the morning.

The trip was brought at length to a successful end. The cargo, or "load," as they called it, was all disposed of for money, the boat itself sold for lumber, and the young men retraced the passage, partly, at least, on shore and on foot, occupying several weeks in the difficult and tedious journey.

Lincoln Splits Several Hundred Rails for a Pair of Pants—How He Looked, as Described by a Companion.

A gentleman by the name of George Cluse, who used to work with Abraham Lincoln during his first years in Illinois, says that at that time he was the roughest looking person he ever saw. He was tall, angular and ungainly, wore trowsers made of flax and tow, cut tight at the ankle and out at both knees. He was known to be very poor, but he was a welcome guest in every house in the neighborhood. Mr. Cluse speaks of splitting rails with Abraham, and reveals some very interesting facts concerning wages. Money was a commodity never reckoned upon. Lincoln split rails to get clothing, and he made a bargain with Mrs. Nancy Miller to split four hundred rails for every yard of brown jeans, dyed with white walnut bark, that would be nescessary to make him a pair of trowsers. In these days Lincoln used to walk five, six, and seven miles to work.

Lincoln's Story of a Girl in New Salem.

Among the numerous delegations which thronged Washington in the early part of the war, was one from New York, which urged very strenuously the sending of a fleet to the southern cities—Charleston, Mobile and Savannah—with the object of drawing off the rebel army from Washington. Mr. Lincoln said the object reminded him of the case of a girl in New Salem, who was greatly troubled with a "singing" in her head. Various remedies were suggested by the neighbors, but nothing tried afforded any relief. At last a man came along—"a common-sense sort of man," said he, inclining his head towards the gentleman complimentarily—"who was asked to prescribe for the difficulty. After due inquiry and examination, he said the cure was very simple.

'What is it?' was the question.

'Make plaster of *psalm-tunes*, and apply to her feet, and draw the "singing" *down*,' was the rejoinder."

Mrs. Brown's Story of Young Abe—How a Man Slept with the President of the United States.

Rev. A. Hale, of Springfield, Ill., is responsible for the following interesting story: Mr. Hale, in May, 1861 (after Lincoln's election to the Presidency), went out about seven miles from his home to visit a sick lady, and found there a Mrs. Brown who had come in as a neighbor. Mr. Lincoln's name having been mentioned, Mrs. Brown said: " Well, I remember Mr. Linken. He worked with my old man thirty-four year ago, and made a crap. We lived on the same farm where we live now, and he worked all the season, and made a crap of corn, and the next Winter they hauled the crap all the way to Galena, and sold it for two dollers and a half a bushel. At that time there was no public houses, and travelers were obliged to stay at any house along the road that could take them in. One evening a right smart looking man rode up to the fence, and asked my old man if he could get to stay over night. ' Well,' said Mr. Brown, ' we can feed your crittur, and give you something to eat, but we can't lodge you unless you can sleep on the same bed with the hired man.' The man hesitated, and asked, ' Where is he?' ' Well, said Mr. Brown, ' you can come and see him.' So the man got down from his crittur, and Mr. Brown took him around to where, in the shade of the house, Mr. Lincoln lay his full length on the ground, with an open book before him. ' There,' said Mr. Brown, pointing at him, ' he is.' The stranger looked at him a minute, and said, ' Well, I think he'll do,' and he staid and slept with the President of the United States."

When and Where Lincoln Obtained the Name of "Honest Abe."

During the year that Lincoln was in Denton Offutt's store, that gentleman, whose business was somewhat widely and unwisely spread about the country, ceased to prosper in his finances, and finally failed. The store was shut up, the mill was closed, and Abraham Lincoln was out of business. The year had been one of great advances, in many respects. He had made new and valuable acquaintances, read many books, mastered the grammar of his own tongue, won multitudes of friends, and become ready for a step still further in advance. Those who could appreciate brains respected him, and those whose highest ideas of a man related to his muscles were devoted to him. Every one trusted him. It was while he was preforming the duties of the store that he acquired the soubriquet "Honest Abe" —a characterization that he never dishonored, and an abbreviation that he never outgrew. He was judge, arbitrator, referee, umpire, authority, in all disputes, games and matches of man-flesh and horse-flesh; a pacificator in all quarrels; everybody's friend; the best natured, the most sensible, the best informed, the most modest and unassuming, the kindest, gentlest, roughest, strongest, best young fellow in all New Salem and the region round about.

Lincoln's Mechanical Ingenuity—His Patent Boat.

That he had enough mechanical genius to make him a good mechanic, there is no doubt. With such rude tools as were at his command he had made cabins and flat-boats; and after his mind had become absorbed in public and professional affairs he often recurred to his mechanical dreams for amusement. One of his dreams took form, and he endeavored to make a practical matter of it. He had had experience in the early navigation of the Western rivers. One of the most serious hinderances to this navigation was low water, and the lodgment of the various craft on the shifting shoals and bars with which these rivers abound. He undertook to contrive an apparatus which, folded to the hull of a boat like a bellows, might be inflated on occasion, and, by its levity, lift it over any obstruction upon which it might rest. On this contrivance, illustrated by a model whittled out by himself, and now preserved in the Patent Office at Washington, he secured letters patent; but it is certain that the navigation of the Western rivers was not revolutionized by it.

A Remarkable Story—"Honest Abe" as Postmaster—How He Kept the Identical Money in Trust for Many Years.

Mr. Lincoln was appointed Postmaster by President Jackson. The office was too insignificant to be considered politically, and it was given to the young man because everybody liked him, and because he was the only man willing to take it who could make out the returns. He was exceedingly pleased with the appointment, because it gave him a chance to read every newspaper that was taken in the vicinity. He had never been able to get half the newspapers he wanted before, and the office gave him the prospect of a constant feast. Not wishing to be tied to the office, as it yielded him no revenue that would reward him for the confinement, he made a Post-office of his hat. Whenever he went out, the letters were placed in his hat. When an anxious looker for a letter found the Postmaster, he had found his office; and the public officer, taking off his hat, looked over his mail wherever the public might find him. He kept the office until it was discontinued, or removed to Petersburg.

One of the most beautiful exhibitions of Mr. Lincoln's rigid honesty occurred in connection with the settlement of his accounts with the Post-office Department, several years afterwards. It was after he had become a lawyer, and had been a legislator. He had passed through a period of great poverty, had acquired his education in the law in the midst of many perplexities, inconveniences, and hardships, and had met with temptations, such as few men could resist, to make a temporary use of any money he might have in his hands. One day, seated in the law office of his partner, the agent of the Post-office Department entered, and inquired if Abraham Lincoln was within. Mr. Lincoln responded to his name, and was informed that the agent had called to collect a balance due the Department since the discontinuance of the New Salem office. A shade of perplexity passed over Mr. Lincoln's face, which did not escape the notice of friends who were present. One of them said at once: "Lincoln, if you are in want of money, let us help you." He made no reply, but suddenly rose, and pulled out from a pile of books a little old trunk, and, returning to the table, asked the agent how much the amount of his debt was. The sum was named, and then Mr. Lincoln opened the trunk, pulled out a little package of coin wrapped in a cotton rag, and *counted out the exact sum,* amounting to something more than seventeen dollars. After the agent had left the room, he remarked quietly that he never used any man's money but his own. Although this sum had been in his hands during all these years, he had never regarded it as available, even for any temporary purpose of his own.

3

How Lincoln Piloted a Flat-Boat Over a Mill-Dam.

Governor Yates, of Illinois, in a speech at Springfield, quoted one of Mr. Lincoln's early friends—W. T. Greene— as having said that the first time he ever saw Mr. Lincoln, he was in the Sangamon River with his trousers rolled up five feet, more or less, trying to pilot a flat-boat over a mill-dam. The boat was so full of water that it was hard to manage. Lincoln got the prow over, and then, instead of waiting to bail the water out, bored a hole through the projecting part and let it run out; affording a forcible illustration of the ready ingenuity of the future President in the quick invention of moral expedients.

Splitting Rails and Studying Mathematics—Simmons, Lincoln & Company.

In the year 1855 or '56, George B. Lincoln, Esq., of Brooklyn, was traveling through the West in connection with a large New York dry-goods establishment. He found himself one night in a town on the Illinois River, by the name of Naples. The only tavern of the place had evidently been constructed with reference to business on a small scale. Poor as the prospect seemed, Mr. Lincoln had no alternative but to put up at the place. The supper-room was also used as a lodging-room. After supper and a comfortable hour before the fire, Mr. L. told his host that he thought he would "go to bed." "Bed!" echoed the landlord ; "there is no bed for you in this house, unless you sleep with that man yonder. He has the only one we have to spare." "Well," returned Mr. Lincoln, "the gentleman has possession, and perhaps would not like a bedfellow." Upon this, a grizzly head appeared out of the pillows, and said, "What is your name?" "They call

EARLY HOME OF THE LINCOLNS IN ILLINOIS.

Located in Macon County, in the Sangamon Valley, about ten miles from Decatur. It was here, during the first year, that Abraham Lincoln and John Hanks split several thousand rails. Lincoln was about twenty years of age at this time.

me Lincoln at home," was the reply. "Lincoln!" repeated the stranger; "any connection of our Illinois Abraham?" "No," replied Mr. L., "I fear not." "Well," said the old man, "I will let any man by the name of 'Lincoln' sleep with me, just for the sake of the name. You have heard of Abe?" he inquired. "Oh, yes, very often," replied Mr. Lincoln. "No man could travel far in this State without hearing of *him*, and I would be very glad to claim connection, if I could do so honestly." "Well," said the old gentleman, "my name is Simmons. 'Abe' and I used to live and work together when we were young men. Many a job of wood-cutting and rail-splitting have I done up with him. Abe Lincoln," said he, with emphasis, "was the *likeliest* boy in God's world. He would work all day as hard as any of us —and study by firelight in the log-house half the night; and in this way he made himself a thorough practical surveyor. Once, during those days, I was in the upper part of the State, and I met General Ewing, whom President Jackson had sent to the Northwest to make surveys. I told him about Abe Lincoln, what a student he was, and that I wanted he should give him a job. He looked over his memoranda, and, pulling out a paper, said: 'There is —— county must be surveyed; if your friend can do the work properly, I shall be glad to have him undertake it— the compensation will be six hundred dollars!' Pleased as I could be, I hastened to Abe, after I got home, with an account of what I had secured for him. He was sitting before the fire in the log-cabin when I told him; and what do you think was his answer? When I finished, he looked up very quietly, and said, 'Mr. Simmons, I thank you very sincerely for your kindness, but I don't think I will undertake the job.' 'In the name of wonder,' said I, 'why? Six hundred dollars does not grow upon every bush out

here in Illinois.' 'I know that,' said Abe, 'and I need
the money bad enough, Simmons, as you know; but I
have never been under obligation to a Democratic administration, and I never intend to be so long as I can get my
living another way. General Ewing must find another
man to do his work.' ' "

Mr. Carpenter related this story to the President one
day, and asked him if it was true. "Pollard Simmons ! "
said Lincoln : "well do I remember him. It is correct
about our working togethe ; but the old man must have
stretched the facts somewhat about the survey of the
county. I think I should have been very glad of the job
at that time, no matter what administration was in power."
Notwithstanding this, however, Mr. Carpenter was inclined
to believe Mr. Simmons was not far out of the way and
thought his statement seemed very characteristic of what
Abraham Lincoln may be supposed to have been at twenty-
three or twenty-five years of age.

Captain Lincoln—How he Became Captain.

In the threatening aspect of affairs at the time of the
Black Hawk War, Governor Reynolds issued a call for
volunteers, and among the companies that immediately
responded was one from Menard County, Illinois. Many
of the volunteers were from New Salem and Clary's
Grove, and Lincoln, being out of business, was the first to
enlist. The company being full, they held a meeting at
Richland for the election of officers. Lincoln had won
many hearts, and they told him that he must be their captain. It was an office that he did not aspire to, and one
for which he felt that he had no special fitness; but he
consented to be a candidate. There was but one other
candidate for the office (a Mr. Kirkpatrick), and he was

one of the most influential men in the county. Previously, Kirkpatrick had been an employer of Lincoln, and was so overbearing in his treatment of the young man that the latter left him.

The simple mode of electing their captain, adopted by the company, was by placing the candidates apart, and telling the men to go and stand with the one they preferred. Lincoln and his competitor took their positions, and then the word was given. At least three out of every four went to Lincoln at once. When it was seen by those who had ranged themselves with the other candidate that Lincoln was the choice of the majority of the company, they left their places, one by one, and came over to the successful side, until Lincoln's opponent in the friendly strife was left standing almost alone. " I felt badly to see him cut so," says a witness of the scene. Here was an opportunity for revenge. The humble laborer was his employer's captain, but the opportunity was never improved. Mr. Lincoln frequently confessed that no subsequent success of his life had given him half the satisfaction that this election did. He had achieved public recognition ; and to one so humbly bred, the distinction was inexpressibly delightful.

A Humorous Speech—Lincoln in the Black Hawk War.

The friends of General Cass, when that gentleman was a candidate for the presidency, endeavored to endow him with a military reputation. Mr. Lincoln, at that time a representative in Congress, delivered a speech before the House, which, in its allusions to General Cass, was exquisitely sarcastic and irresistiby humorous :

"By the way, Mr. Speaker," said Mr. Lincoln, " do **you** know I am a military hero ? Yes, sir, in the days

of the Black Hawk War, I fought, bled and came away.
Speaking of General Cass' career remin's me of my own.
I was not at Stillman's Defeat, but I was about as near it
as Cass to Hull's surrender; and like him I saw the
place very soon afterward. It is quite certain I did not
break my sword, for I had none to break; but I bent my
musket pretty badly on one occasion. * * * * If
General Cass went in advance of me in picking whortle-
berries, I guess I surpassed him in charges upon the wild
onions. If he saw any live, fighting Indians, it was more
than I did, but I had a good many bloody struggles with
the musquitoes; and although I never fainted from loss of
blood, I can truly say I was often very hungry." Mr. Lincoln concluded by saying if he ever turned democrat and
should run for the Presidency, he hoped they would not
make fun of him by attempting to make him a military
hero !

Lincoln's First Political Speech.

Mr. Lincoln made his first political speech in 1832, at
the age of twenty-three, when he was a candidate for the
Illinois Legislature. His opponent had wearied the audience by a long speech, leaving him but a short time in
which to present his views. He condensed all he had to
say into a few words, as follows :

"Gentlemen, Fellow-citizens : I presume you know who
1 am. I am humble Abraham Lincoln. I have been
solicited by many friends to become a candidate for the
legislature. My politics can be briefly stated. I am in
favor of the internal improvement system, and a high
protective tariff. These are my sentiments and political
principles. If elected, I shall be thankful. If not, it
will be all the same."

Elected to the Legislature—Lincoln Walks to the State Capitol, Distant 100 Miles!

In 1834, Lincoln was a candidate for the legislature, and was elected by the highest vote cast for any candidate. Major John T. Stuart, an officer in the Black Hawk War, and whose acquaintance Lincoln made at Beardstown, was also elected. Major Stuart had already conceived the highest opinion of the young man, and seeing much of him during the canvass for the election, privately advised him to study law. Stuart was himself engaged in a large and lucrative legal practice at Springfield. Lincoln said he was poor—that he had no money to buy books, or to live where books might be borrowed and used. Major Stuart offered to lend him all he needed, and he decided to take the kind lawyer's advice, and accept his offer. At the close of the canvass which resulted in his election, he walked to Springfield, borrowed "a load" of books of Stuart, and took them home with him to New Salem. Here he began the study of law in good earnest, though with no preceptor. He studied while he had bread, and then started out on a surveying tour, to win the money that would buy more. One who remembers his habits during this period says that he went, day after day, for weeks, and sat under an oak tree on a hill near New Salem and read, moving around to keep in the shade, as the sun moved. He was so much absorbed that some people thought and said that he was crazy. Not unfrequently he met and passed his best friends without noticing them. The truth was that he had found the pursuit of his life, and had become very much in earnest.

During Lincoln's campaign, he possessed and rode a horse, to procure which he had quite likely sold his compass and chain, for, as soon as the canvass had closed, he sold the horse, and bought these instruments indispensable to him in the only pursuit by which he could make his living. When the time for the assembling of the legislature approached, Lincoln dropped his law books, shouldered his pack, and, on foot, trudged to Vandalia, then the capital of the State, about a hundred miles, to make his entrance into public life.

"The Long Nine"—Lincoln the Longest of All.

The Sangamon County delegation to the Illinois Legislature, in 1834, of which Lincoln was a member, consisting of nine representatives, was so remarkable for the physical altitude of its members that they were known as "The Long Nine." Not a member of the number was less than six feet high, and Lincoln was the tallest of the nine, as he was the leading man intellectually, in and out of the House. Among those who composed the House, were General John A. McClernand, afterwards a member of Congress; Jesse K. Dubois, afterwards Auditor of the State; James Semple, afterwards twice the Speaker of the House of Representatives, and subsequently United States Senator; Robert Smith, afterwards member of Congress; John Hogan, afterwards a member of Congress from St. Louis; General James Shields, afterwards United States Senator (who died recently); John Dement, who has since been Treasurer of the State; Stephen A. Douglas, whose subsequent public career is familiar to all; Newton Cloud, President of the Convention which framed the present State Constitution of Illinois; John J. Hardin, who fell at Buena Vista; John Moore, afterwards Lieutenant Governor of the State; William A. Richardson, subsequently United States Senator, and William McMurtry, who has since been Lieutenant Governor of the State. This list does not embrace all who had then, or who have since been distinguished, but it is large enough to show that Lincoln was, during the term of this legislature, thrown into association, and often into antagonism, with the brightest men of the new state.

Returning from the Legislature—" No Wonder Lincoln was Cold"— A Joke on Lincoln's Big Feet.

He had walked his hundred miles to Vandalia, in 1836, as he did in 1834, and when the session closed he walked home again. A gentleman in Menard County remembers meeting him and a detachment of " The Long Nine " on their way home. They were all mounted except Lincoln, who had thus far kept up with them on foot. If he had money he was hoarding it for more important purposes than that of saving leg-weariness and leather. The weather was raw, and Lincoln's clothing were none of the warmest. Complaining of being cold to one of his companions, this irreverent member of " The Long Nine " told his future President that it was no wonder he was cold—" there was so much of him on the ground." None of the party appreciated this homely joke at the expense of his feet (they were doubtless able to bear it) more thoroughly than Lincoln himself. We can imagine the cross-fires of wit and humor by which the way was enlivened during this cold and tedious journey. The scene was certainly a rude one, and seems more like a dream than a reality, when we remember that it occurred not very many years ago, in a state which now contains hardly less than three millions of people and seven thousand six hundred miles of railway.

Lincoln's Marriage—Boarding at $4 per Week—Some Very Interest-
ng Letters—A Peep into Lincoln's Social Life.

In 1842, in his thirty-third year, Mr. Lincoln married
Miss Mary Todd, a daughter of Hon. Robert S. Todd, of
Lexington, Kentucky. The marriage took place in Springfield, where the lady had for several years resided, on the
fourth of November of the year mentioned. It is probable
that he married as early as the circumstances of his life permitted, for he had always loved the society of women, and
possessed a nature that took profound delight in intimate
female companionship. A letter written on the eighteenth
of May following his marriage, to J. F. Speed, Esq., of
Louisville, Kentucky, an early and a life-long personal friend,
gives a pleasant glimpse of his domestic arrangements at
this time. "We are not keeping house," Mr. Lincoln says
in this letter, " but boarding at the Globe Tavern, which is
very well kept now by a widow lady of the name of Beck.
Our rooms are the same Dr. Wallace occupied there, and
boarding only costs four dollars a week. * * * I most
heartily wish you and your Fanny will not fail to come.
Just let us know the time, a week in advance, and we will
have a room prepared for you, and we'll all be merry together
for awhile." He seems to have been in excellent spirits, and
to have been very hearty in the enjoyment of his new relation. The private letters of Mr. Lincoln were charmingly
natural and sincere. His personal friendships were the
sweetest sources of his happiness.

To a particular friend, he wrote February 25, 1842:
"Yours of the sixteenth, announcing that Miss —— and
you 'are no longer twain, but one flesh,' reached me this
morning. I have no way of telling you how much happiness I wish you both, though I believe you both can con-
ceive it. I feel somewhat jealous of both of you now, for

you will be so exclusively concerned for one another that I shall be forgotten entirely. My acquaintance with Miss —— (I call her thus lest you should think I am speaking of your mother,) was too short for me to reasonably hope to long be remembered by her; and still I am sure I shall not forget her soon. Try if you can not remind her of that debt she owes me, and be sure you do not interfere to pre-vent her paying it.

"I regret to learn that you have resolved not to return to Illinois. I shall be very lonesome without you. How mis-erably things seem to be arranged in this world! If we have no friends we have no pleasure; and we have them, we are sure to lose them, and be doubly pained by the loss. I did hope she and you would make your home here, yet I own I have no right to insist. You owe obligations to her ten thousand times more sacred than any you can owe to others, and in that light let them be respected and observed. It is natural that she should desire to remain with her rela-tions and friends. As to friends, *she* could not need them anywhere—she would have them in abundance here. Give my kind regards to Mr. —— and his family, particularly to Miss E. Also to your mother, brothers and sisters. Ask little E. D—— if she will ride to town with me if I come there again. And, finally, give —— a double reciprocation of all the love she sent me. Write me often, and believe me, yours forever, LINCOLN.

Lincoln's Mother—How He Loved Her.

"A great man," says J. G. Holland, "never drew his infant life from a purer or more womanly bosom than her own; and Mr. Lincoln always looked back to her with an unspeakable affection. Long after her sensitive heart and weary hands had crumbled into dust, and had climbed to

life again in forest flowers, he said to a friend, with tears in
his eyes: ' All that I am, or hope to be, I owe to my angel
mother—blessings on her memory!' " She was five feet,
five inches high, a slender, pale, sad and sensitive woman,
with much in her nature that was truly heroic, and much
that shrank from the rude life around her. Her death
occurred in 1818, scarcely two years after her removal from
Kentucky to Indiana, and when Abraham was in his tenth
year. They laid her to rest under the trees near their
cabin home, and, sitting on her grave, the little boy wept
his irreparable loss.

Gen. Linder's Early Recollections of Lincoln—Some Amusing Stories of Lincoln's Uncle Mord.

I did not travel, says General Linder, on the circuit in
1835, on account of my health and the health of my wife,
but attended court at Charleston that Fall, held by Judge
Grant, who had exchanged circuits with our judge, Justin
Harlan. It was here I first met Abraham Lincoln, of
Springfield, at that time a very modest and retiring man,
dressed in a plain suit of mixed jeans. He did not make
any marked impression upon me, or any other member of
the bar. He was on a visit to his relations in Coles, where
his father and stepmother lived, and some of her children.
Lincoln put up at the hotel, and here was where I saw him
Whether he was reading law at this time I can not say.
Certain it is, he had not been admitted to the bar, although
he had some celebrity, having been a captain in the Black-
Hawk campaign, and served a term in the Illinois Legislature; but if he won any fame at that season I have never
heard of it. He had been one of the representatives from
Sangamon. If Lincoln at this time felt the divine afflatus
of greatness stir within him I have never heard of it. It

was rather common among us then in the West to suppose that there was no Presidential timber growing in the North-west, yet, he doubtless had at that time the stuff out of which to make half a dozen Presidents.

I had known his relatives in Kentucky, and he asked me about them. His uncle, Mordecai Lincoln, I had known form my boyhood, and he was naturally a man of consider-able genius; he was a man of great drollery, and it would almost make you laugh to look at him. I never saw but one other man whose quiet, droll look excited in me the same disposition to laugh, and that was Artemas Ward. He was quite a story-teller, and in this Abe resembled his Uncle Mord, as we all called him. He was an honest man, as tender-hearted as a woman, and to the last degree charit-able and benevolent.

No one ever took offense at Uncle Mord's stories—not even the ladies. I heard him once tell a bevy of fashion able girls that he knew a very large woman who had a hus band so small that in the night she often mistook him for the baby, and that upon one occasion she took him up and was singing to him a soothing lullaby, when he awoke and told her that she was mistaken, that the baby was on the other side of the bed.

Lincoln had a very high opinion of his uncle, and on one occasion he said to me: "Linder, I have often said that Uncle Mord had run off with the talents of the family."

Old Mord, as we sometimes called him, had been in his younger days a very stout man, and was quite fond of play-ing a game of fisticuffs with any one who was noted as a champion. He told a parcel of us once of a pitched battle he had fought with one of the champions of that day. He said they fought on the side of a hill or ridge; that at the bottom there was a rut or canal, which had been cut out by the freshets. He said they soon clinched, and he threw his man and fell on top of him.   He said he always thought he had the best eyes in the world for measuring distances, and having measured the distance to the bottom of the hill, he concluded that by rolling over and over till they came to the bottom his antagonist's body would fill it, and he would be wedged in so tight that he could whip him at his leisure. So he let the fellow turn him, and over and over they went, when about the twentieth revolution brought Uncle Mord's back in contact with the bottom of the rut, "and," said he, " before fire could scorch a feather, I cried out in stentorian voice: ' Take him off!' "

Young Lincoln and the " Clary's Grove Boys "—A Wrestling Match and How it Terminated.

There lived at the time young Lincoln resided at New Salem, Illinois, in and around the village, a band of rollicking fellows, or, more properly, roystering rowdies, known as the " Clary's Grove Boys." The special tie that united them was physical courage and prowess. These fellows, although they embraced in their number many men who have since become respectable and influential, were wild and rough beyond toleration in any community not made up like that which produced them. They pretended to be " regulators," and were the terror of all who did not acknowledge their rule; and their mode of securing allegiance was by flogging every man who failed to acknowledge it. They took it upon themselves to try the mettle of every new comer, and to learn the sort of stuff he was made of. Some of their number was appointed to fight, wrestle, or run a foot-race with each incoming stranger. Of course Abraham Lincoln was obliged to pass the ordeal.

Perceiving that he was a man who would not easily be floored, they selected their champion, Jack Armstrong, and imposed upon him the task of laying Lincoln upon his back. There is no evidence that Lincoln was an unwilling party in the sport, for it was what he had always been accustomed to. The bout was entered upon, but Armstrong soon discovered that he had met with more than his match. The "Boys" were looking on, and, seeing that their champion was likely to get the worst of it, did after the manner of such irresponsible bands. They gathered around Lincoln, struck and disabled him, and then Armstrong, by "legging" him, got him down.

Most men would have been indignant, not to say furiously angry, under such foul treatment as this; but if Lincoln was either, he did not show it. Getting up in perfect good humor, he fell to laughing over his discomfiture, and joking about it. They had all calculated upon making him angry, and then they intended, with the amiable spirit which characterized the "Clary's Grove Boys," to give him a terrible drubbing. They were disappointed, and, in their admiration of him, immediately invited him to become one of the company.

A Batch of Lincoln Reminiscences — The Turning Point in the Great Man's Life.

It was while young Lincoln was engaged in the duties of Offutt's store that the turning point in his life occurred Here he commenced the study of English grammar. There was not a text-book to be obtained in the neighborhood, but, hearing that there was a copy of Kirkham's Grammar in the possession of a person seven or eight miles distant, he walked to his house and succeeded in borrowing it.

L. M. Green, a lawyer of Petersburg, in Menard County, says that every time he visited New Salem, at this period, Lincoln took him out upon a hill, and *asked him to explain some point* in Kirkham that had given him trouble. After having mastered the book, he remarked to a friend, that if that was what they called a science, he thought he could "*subdue another.*"

Mr. Green says that Mr. Lincoln's talk at this time showed that he was beginning to think of a great life and a great destiny. Lincoln said to him, on one occasion, that all his family seemed to have good sense, but, somehow, none had ever become distinguished. He thought that perhaps he might become so. He had talked, he said, with men who had the reputation of being great men, but he could not see that they *differed much from others!*

During this year, he was also much engaged with debating clubs, often walking six or seven miles to attend them. One of these clubs held its meetings at an old store-house in New Salem, and the first speech young Lincoln ever made was made there. He used to call the exercise "practicing polemics." As these clubs were composed principally of men of no education whatever, some of their "polemics" are remembered as the most laughable of farces.

His favorite newspaper, at this time, was the Louisville *Journal*, a paper which he received regularly by mail, and paid for during a number of years when he had not money enough to dress decently. He liked its politics, and was particularly delighted with its wit and humor, of which he had the keenest appreciation. When out of the store, he was always busy in the pursuit of knowledge.

One gentleman who met him during this period, says that the first time he saw him he was lying on a trundle-bed, covered with books and papers, and *rocking a cradle with his foot.* The whole scene, however, was entirely characteristic—Lincoln reading and studying, and at the same time helping his landlady by quieting her child.

" My early history," said Mr. Lincoln to J. L. Scripps, " ⌣ perfectly characterized by a single line of Gray's Elegy:

'The short and simple annals of the poor.' "

A GENTLEMAN who knew Mr. Lincoln well in early manhood says: " Lincoln at this period had nothing but *plenty of friends.*"

SAYS J. G. Holland: "No man ever lived, probably, who was more a self-made man than Abraham Lincoln. Not a circumstance of life favored the development which he had reached."

IN his seventh year Lincoln attended his first school. Zacharia Riney, a Catholic, whose memory Lincoln always revered, was the teacher. Caleb Hazel was the second teacher, under whose instructions Lincoln learned to write a good legible hand in three months.

AFTER the customary hand-shaking, on one occasion at Washington, several gentlemen came forward and asked the President for his autograph. One of them gave his name as " Cruikshank." " That reminds me," said Mr. Lincoln, " of what I used to be called when a young man— ' *Long-shanks!*' "

MR. HOLLAND says: " Lincoln was a religious man. The fact may be stated without any reservation—with only an explanation. He believed in God, and in His personal supervision of the affairs of men. He believed himself to be under His control and guidance. He believed in the power and ultimate triumph of the right, through his belief in God."

GOVERNOR YATES, in a speech at Springfield, before a meeting at which William G. Greene presided, quoted Mr. Greene as having said that the first time he ever saw Lincoln he was "in the Sangamon River, with his trousers rolled up five feet more or less, trying to pilot a flat-boat over a mill-dam. The boat was so full of water that it was hard to manage. Lincoln got the prow over, and then, instead of waiting to bail the water out, bored a hole through the projecting part, *and let it run out.*"

A PROMINENT writer says: " Lincoln was a child-like man. No public man of modern days has been fortunate enough to carry into his manhood so much of the directness, truthfulness, and simplicity of childhood as distinguished him. *He was exactly what he seemed.*

MR. LINCOLN and Douglas met for the first time when the latter was only 23 years of age. Lincoln, in speaking of the fact, subsequently said that Douglas was then " the least man he ever saw." He was not only very short, but very slender.

LINCOLN's mother died in 1818, scarcely two years after her removal to Indiana from Kentucky, and when Abraham was in his tenth year. They laid her to rest under the trees near the cabin, and, sitting on her grave, the little boy wept his irreparable loss.

THE Black Hawk war was not a very remarkable affair. It made no military reputations, but it was noteworthy in the single fact that the two simplest, homliest and truest men engaged in it afterward became Presidents of the United States, viz: General (then Colonel) Zachary Taylor, and Abraham Lincoln. Mr. Lincoln never spoke of it as anything more than an interesting episode in his life, except upon one occasion when he used it as an instrument for turning the military pretensions of another into ridicule.

STATE CAPITOL AT SPRINGFIELD, ILL.

PROFESSIONAL LIFE STORIES.

How Lincoln and Judge B—— Swapped Horses.

When Abraham Lincoln was a lawyer in Illinois, he and a certain Judge once got to bantering one another about trading horses; and it was agreed that the next morning at 9 o'clock they should make a trade, the horses to be unseen up to that hour, and no backing out, under a forfeiture of $25.

At the hour appointed the Judge came up, leading the sorriest-looking specimen of a horse ever seen in those parts. In a few minutes Mr. Lincoln was seen approaching with a wooden saw-horse upon his shoulders. Great were the shouts and the laughter of the crowd, and both were greatly increased when Mr. Lincoln, on surveying the Judge's animal, set down his saw-horse, and exclaimed: "Well, Judge, this is the first time I ever got the worst of it in a horse trade."

A Remarkable Law Suit About a Colt—How Lincoln Won the Case—Thirty-Four Men Against Thirty Men and Two Brutes.

The controversy was about a colt, in which thirty-four witnesses swore that they had known the colt from its falling, and that it was the property of the plaintiff, while thirty swore that they had known the colt from its falling, and that it was the property of the defendant. It may be stated, at starting, that these witnesses were all honest, and that the mistake grew out of the exact resemblances which two colts bore to each other.

One circumstance was proven by all the witnesses, or nearly all of them, viz.: that the two claimants of the colt agreed to meet on a certain day with the two mares which were respectively claimed to be the dams of the colt, and permit the colt to decide which of the two he belonged to. The meeting occurred according to agreement, and, as it was a singular case and excited a good deal of popular interest, there were probably a hundred men assembled on their horses and mares, from far and near.

Now, the colt really belonged to the defendant in the case. It had strayed away and fallen into company with the plaintiff's horses. The plaintiff's colt had, at the same time, strayed away, and had not returned, and was not to be found. The moment the two mares were brought upon the ground, the defendant's mare and the colt gave signs of recognition. The colt went to its dam, and would not leave her. They fondled each other ; and, although the plaintiff brought his mare between them, and tried in various ways to divert the colt's attention, the colt would not be separated from its dam. It then followed her home, a distance of eight or ten miles, and, when within a mile or two of the stables, took a short cut to them in advance of its dam. The plaintiff had sued to recover the colt thus gone back to its owner.

In the presentation of this case to the jury, there were thirty-four witnesses on the side of the plaintiff, while the defendant had, on his side, only thirty witnesses; but he had on his side the colt itself and its dam—thirty-four men against thirty men and two brutes. Here was a case that was to be decided by the preponderance of evidence. All the witnesses were equally positive, and equally credible. Mr. Lincoln was on the side of the defendant, and contended that the voice of nature in the mare and colt ought to outweigh the testimony of a hundred men. The jury were all farmers, and all illiterate men, and he took great pains to make them understand what was meant by the " preponderance of evidence." He said that in a civil suit, absolute certainty, or such certainty as would be required to convict a man of crime, was not essential. They must decide the case according to the impression which the evidence had produced upon their minds, and, if they felt puzzled at all, he would give them a test by which they could bring themselves to a just conclusion. " Now," said he, "if you were going to bet on this case, on which side would you be willing to risk a picayune? That side on which you would be willing to bet a picayune, is the side on which rests the preponderance of evidence in your minds. It is possible that you may not be right, but that is not the question. The question is as to where the preponderance of evidence lies, and you can judge exactly where it lies in your minds, by deciding as to which side you would be willing to bet on."

The jury understood this. There was no mystification about it. They had got hold of a test by which they could render an intelligent verdict. Mr. Lincoln saw into their minds, and knew exactly what they needed; and the moment they received it, he knew that his case was safe, as a quick verdict for the defendant proved it to be. In nothing connected with this case was the ingenuity of Mr. Lincoln more evident, perhaps, than in the insignificance of the sum which he placed in risk by the hypothetical wager. It was not a hundred dollars, or a thousand dollars, or even a dollar, but the smallest silver coin, to show to them that the verdict should go with the preponderance of evidence, even if the preponderance should be only a hair's weight.

Lincoln's Story of a Young Lawyer as He Told it to General Garfield.

General Garfield, of Ohio, received from the President the account of the capture of Norfolk with the following preface: " By the way, Garfield," said Mr. Lincoln, " you never heard, did you, that Chase, Stanton, and I, had a campaign of our own? We went down to Fortress Monroe in Chase's revenue cutter, and consulted with Admiral Goldsborough as to the feasibility of taking Norfolk by landing on the north shore and making a march of eight miles. The Admiral said, very positively, there was no landing on that shore, and we should have to double the cape and approach the place from the south side, which would be a long and difficult journey. I thereupon asked him if he had ever tried to find a landing, and he replied that he had not.

" ' Now,' said I, ' Admiral, that reminds me of a chap out West who had studied law, but had never tried a case. Being sued, and not having confidence in his ability to manage his own case, he employed a fellow-lawyer to manage it for him. He had only a confused idea of the meaning of law terms, but was anxious to make a display of learning, and on the trial constantly made suggestions to his lawyer, who paid no attention to him. At last, fearing that his lawyer was not handling the opposing counsel very well, he lost all patience, and, springing to his feet, cried out: " Why don't you go at him with a *capias*, or a *surre-butter*, or something, and not stand there like a confounded old *nudum-pactum?*"

Lincoln and His Step-Mother—How He Bought Her a Farm.

Soon after Mr. Lincoln entered upon his profession at Springfield, he was engaged in a criminal case in which it was thought there was little chance of success. Throwing all his powers into it he came off victorious, and promptly received for his services five hundred dollars. A legal friend calling upon him the next morning found him sitting before a table, upon which his money was spread out, counting it over and over.

"Look here, Judge," said Lincoln; "See what a heap of money I've got from the —— case. Did you ever see anything like it? Why, I never had so much money in my life before, put it all together?" Then crossing his arms upon the table, his manner sobering down, he added, "I have got just five hundred dollars : if it were only seven hundred and fifty, I would go directly and purchase a quarter section of land, and settle it upon my old step-mother."

His friend said that if the deficiency was all he needed he would loan him the amount, taking his note, to which Mr. Lincoln instantly acceded.

His friend then said : "Lincoln, I would not do just what you have indicated. Your step-mother is getting old, and will not probably live many years. I would settle the property upon her for her use during her lifetime, to revert to you upon her death."

With much feeling, Mr. Lincoln replied: "I shall do no such thing. It is a poor return, at the best, for all the good woman's devotion and fidelity to me, and there is not going to be any half-way business about it ;" and so saying, he gathered up his money and proceeded forthwith to carry his long-cherished purpose into execution.

A Famous Story—How Lincoln was Presented with a Knife!

It is said that Mr. Lincoln was always ready to join in a laugh at the expense of his person, concerning which he was indifferent. Many of his friends will recognize the following story—the incident having actually occurred—which Lincoln always told with great glee :

" In the days when I used to be ' on the circuit,' " said Lincoln, " I was accosted in the cars by a stranger, who said :

" ' Excuse me, sir, but I have an article in my possession which belongs to you.'

" ' How is that ? ' I asked, considerably astonished.

" The stranger took a jack-knife from his pocket. ' This knife,' said he, ' was placed in my hands some years ago, with the injunction that I was to keep it until I found a man *uglier* than myself. I have carried it from that time to this. Allow me *now* to say, sir, that I think *you* are fairly entitled to the property.' "

An Amusing Story Concerning Thompson Campbell.

Among the numerous visitors on one of the President's reception days, were a party of Congressmen, among whom was the Hon. Thomas Shannon, of California. Soon after the customary greeting, Mr. Shannon said :

" Mr. President, I met an old friend of yours in California last Summer, Thompson Campbell, who had a good deal to say of your Springfield life."

" Ah !" returned Mr. Lincoln, "I am glad to hear of him. Campbell used to be a dry fellow," he continued. " For a time he was Secretary of State. One day, during the legislative vacation, a meek, cadaverous-looking man, with a white neck-cloth, introduced himself to him at his office, and, stating that he had been informed that Mr. C. had the letting of the Assembly Chamber, said that he wished to secure it, if possible, for a course of lectures he desired to deliver in Springfield.

" ' May I ask,' said the Secretary, ' what is to be the subject of your lectures ? '

" ' Certainly,' was the reply, with a very solemn expression of countenance. ' The course I wish to deliver, is on the Second Coming of our Lord.'

" ' It is of no use,' said C. ' If you will take my advice, you will not waste your time in this city. It is my private opinion that if the Lord has been in Springfield *once*, He will not come the *second time !* ' "

The Lincoln-Shields Duel—How it Originated.

The late Gen. Shields was Auditor of the State of Illinois in 1839. While he occupied this important office he was involved in an " affair of honor " with a Springfield lawyer—no less a personage than Abraham Lincoln. At this time " James Shields, Auditor," was the pride of the young Democracy, and was considered a dashing fellow by all, the ladies included. In the Summer of 1842 the Springfield *Journal* contained some letters from the " Lost Townships," by a contributor whose nom de plume was " Aunt Becca," which held up the gallant young Auditor as " a ball-room dandy, floatin' about on the earth without heft or substance, just like a lot of cat-fur where cats had been fightin'."

These letters caused intense excitement in the town. Nobody knew or guessed their authorship. Shields swore it would be coffee and pistols for two if he should find out who had been lampooning him so unmercifully. Thereupon " Aunt Becca " wrote another letter, which made the furnace of his wrath seven times hotter than before, in which

she made a very humble apology, and offered to let him
squeeze her hand for satisfaction, adding:

" If this should not answer, there is one thing more I
would rather do than to get a lickin'. I have all along
expected to die a widow; but, as Mr. Shields is rather good-
looking than otherwise, I must say I don't care if we com-
promise the matter by—really, Mr. Printer, I can't help
blushin'—but I—must come out—I—but widowed modesty
—well, if I must, I must—wouldn't he—maybe sorter le
the old grudge drap if I was to consent to be—be—his wife
I know he is a fightin' man, and would rather fight than eat;
but isn't marryin' better than fightin', though it does sometimes run into it? And I don't think, upon the whole, I'd
be sich a bad match, neither; I'm not over sixty, and am
jest four feet three in my bare feet, and not much more
round the girth; and for color, I wouldn't turn my back to
nary a girl in the Lost Townships. But, after all, maybe
I'm countin' my chickens before they're hatched, and
dreamin' of matrimonial bliss when the only alternative
reserved for me maybe a lickin'. Jeff tells me the way
these fire-eaters do is to give the challenged party the choice
of weapons, which, being the case, I tell you in confidence,
I never fight with anything but broomsticks or hot water,
or a shovelful of coals or some such thing; the former of
which, being somewhat like a shillelah, may not be so very
objectionable to him. I will give him a choice, however,
in one thing, and that is whether, when we fight, I shall
wear breeches or he petticoats, for I presume this change
is sufficient to place us on an equality."

Of course some one had to shoulder the responsibility of
these letters after such a shot. The real author was none
other than Miss Mary Todd, afterward the wife of Abraham
Lincoln, to whom she was engaged, and who was in honor
bound to assume, for belligerent purposes, the responsibil-

ity of her sharp pen-thrusts. Mr. Lincoln accepted the situation. Not long after the two men, with their seconds, were on their way to the field of honor. But the affair was fixed up without any fighting, and thus ended in a fizzle the Lincoln-Shields duel of the Lost Townships.

Lincoln's Story of Joe Wilson and His " Spotted Animals "—Slow Progress in Killing Cats.

Although the friendly relations which existed between the President and Secretary Cameron were not interrupted by the retirement of the latter from the War Office, so important a change in the Administration could not of course take place without the irrepressible " story" from Mr. Lincoln. Shortly after this event some gentlemen called upon the President, and expressing much satisfaction at the change, intimated that in their judgment the interests of the country required an entire reconstruction of the Cabinet.

Mr. Lincoln heard them through, and then shaking his head dubiously, replied, with his peculiar smile: " Gentlemen, when I was a young man I used to know very well one Joe Wilson, who built himself a log-cabin not far from where I lived. Joe was very fond of eggs and chickens, and he took a good deal of pains in fitting up a poultry shed. Having at length got together a choice lot of young fowls —of which he was very proud—he began to be much annoyed by the depredations of those little black and white spotted animals, which it is not necessary to name. One night Joe was awakened by an unusual cackling and fluttering among his chickens. Getting up, he crept out to see what was going on.

" It was a moonlight night, and he soon caught sight of half a dozen of the little pests, which, with their dam, were running in and out of the shadow of the shed. Very wrathy, Joe put a double charge into his old musket, and thought he would 'clean' out the whole tribe at one shot. Somehow he only killed *one*, and the balance scampered off across the field. In telling the story, Joe would always pause here, and hold his nose.

"'Why didn't you follow them up, and kill the rest?' inquired the neighbors.

"'Blast it,' said Joe, 'why, it was eleven weeks before I got over killin' *one*. If you want any more skirmishing in that line you can just do it yourselves!'"

An Incident Related by One of Lincoln's Clients.

It was not possible for Mr. Lincoln to regard his clients simply in the light of business. An unfortunate man was a subject of his sympathy, a Mr. Cogdal, who related the incident to Mr. Holland, met with a financial wreck in 1843. He employed Mr. Lincoln as his lawyer, and at the close of the business, gave him a note to cover the regular lawyer's fees. He was soon afterwards blown up by an accidental discharge of powder, and lost his hand. Meeting Mr. Lincoln some time after the accident, on the steps of the State House, the kind lawyer asked him how he was getting along.

"Badly enough," replied Mr. Cogdal, "I am both broken up in business and crippled." Then he added, "I have been thinking about that note of yours."

Mr. Lincoln, who had probably known all about Mr. Cogdal's troubles, and had prepared himself for the meeting, took out his pocket-book, and saying, with a laugh, "well, you needn't think any more about it," handed him the note.

Mr. Cogdal protesting, Mr. Lincoln said, "if you had the money, I would not take it," and hurried away.

At this same date, he was frankly writing about his poverty to his friends, as a reason for not making them a visit, and probably found it no easy task to take care of his family, even when board at the Globe Tavern was "only four dollars a week."

Lincoln's Valor—He Defends Col. Baker.

On one occasion when Col. Baker was speaking in a court-house, which had been a store-house, and, on making some remarks that were offensive to certain political rowdies in the crowd, they cried : "Take him off the stand." Immediate confusion ensued, and there was an attempt to carry the demand into execution. Directly over the speaker's head was an old scuttle, at which it appeared Mr. Lincoln had been listening to the speech. In an instant, Mr. Lincoln's feet came through the scuttle, followed by his tall and sinewy frame, and he was standing by Colonel Baker's side. He raised his hand, and the assembly subsided immediately into silence.

"Gentlemen," said Mr. Lincoln, "let us not disgrace the age and country in which we live. This is a land where freedom of speech is guaranteed. Mr. Baker has a right to speak, and ought to be permitted to do so. I am here to protect him, and no man shall take him from this stand if I can prevent it."

The suddenness of his appearance, his perfect calmness and fairness, and the knowledge that he would do what he had promised to do, quieted all disturbance, and the speaker concluded his remarks without difficulty.

5

The Judge and the Drunken Coachman.

Attorney-General Bates was once remonstrating with the President against the appointment to a judicial position of considerable importance of a western man, who, though on the " bench," was of indifferent reputation as a lawyer.

"Well now, Judge," returned Mr. Lincoln, "I think you are rather too hard on ——. Besides that, I must tell you, he did me a good turn long ago. When I took to the law, I was walking to court one morning, with some ten or twelve miles of bad road before me, when —— overtook me in his wagon.

" 'Hallo, Lincoln !' said he ; ' going to the court-house? Come in and I will give you a seat.'

"Well, I got in, and —— went on reading his papers. Presently the wagon struck a stump on one side of the road ; then it hopped off to the other. I looked out and saw the driver was jerking from side to side in his seat : so said I, ' Judge, I think your coachman has been taking a drop too much this morning.'

" 'Well, I declare, Lincoln,' said he, ' I should not much wonder if you are right, for he has nearly upset me half-a-dozen times since starting. So, putting his head out of the window, he shouted, ' *Why you infernal scoundrel, you are drunk !* '

"Upon which pulling up his horses and turning round with great gravity, the coachman said ' Be dad ! but that's the first *rightful decision your honor has given for the last twelve months!* ' "

Honest Abe and his Lady Client.

About the time Mr. Lincoln began to be known as a successful lawyer, he was waited upon by a lady, who held a real-estate claim which she desired to have him prosecute, putting into his hands, with the necessary papers, a check for two hundred and fifty dollars, as a retaining fee. Mr. Lincoln said he would look the case over, and asked her to call again the next day. Upon presenting herself, Mr. Lincoln told her that he had gone through the papers very carefully, and he must tell her frankly that there was not a " peg " to hang her claim upon, and he could not conscientiously advise her to bring an action. The lady was satisfied, and, thanking him, rose to go.

" Wait," said Mr. Lincoln, fumbling in his vest pocket; " here is the check you left with me."

" But, Mr. Lincoln," returned the lady, " I think you have earned *that*."

" No, no," he responded, handing it back to her; " that would not be right. I can't take *pay* for doing my duty."

Attention Shown to Relatives — Lincoln and " His Sisters and His Cousins and His Aunts."

One of the most beautiful traits of Mr. Lincoln was his considerate regard for the poor and obscure relatives he had left, plodding along in their humble ways of life. Wherever upon his circuit he found them, he always went to their dwellings, ate with them, and, when convenient, made their houses his home. He never assumed in their presence the slightest superiority to them, in the facts and conditions of his life. He gave them money when they needed and he possessed it. Countless times he was known to leave his companions at the village hotel, after a hard day's work in the court room, and spend the evening with these old

friends and companions of his humbler days. On one
occasion, when urged not to go, he replied, "Why, aunt's
heart would be broken if I should leave town without calling upon her;" yet he was obliged to walk several miles to
make the call.

How Lincoln Kept His Business Accounts—His Remarkable Honesty.

A little fact in Lincoln's Work will illustrate his ever.
present desire to deal honestly and justly with men. He
had always a partner in his professional life, and, when he
went out upon the circuit, this partner was usually at home.
While out, he frequently took up and disposed of cases that
were never entered at the office. In these cases, after
receiving his fees, he divided the money in his pocket-book,
labeling each sum (wrapped in a piece of paper), that
belonged to his partner, stating his name, and the case on
which it was received. He could not be content to keep
an account. He divided the money, so that if he, by any
casualty, should fail of an opportunity to pay it over, there
could be no dispute as to the exact amount that was his
partner's due. This may seem trivial, nay, boyish, but it
was like Mr. Lincoln.

Lincoln in Court.

Senator McDonald states that he saw a jury trial in
Illinois, at which Lincoln defended an old man charged
with assault and battery. No blood had been spilled, but
there was malice in the prosecution, and the chief witness
was eager to make the most of it. On cross-examination,
Lincoln gave him rope and drew him out; asked him how
long the fight lasted, and how much ground it covered.

The witness thought the fight must have lasted half an hour, and covered an acre of ground. Lincoln called his attention to the fact that nobody was hurt, and then, with an inimitable air, asked him if he didn't think it was "*a mighty small crop for an acre of ground.*" The jury rejected the case with contempt as beneath the dignity of twelve brave, good men and true.

In another cause the son of his old friend, who had employed him and loaned him books, was charged with a murder committed in a riot at a camp-meeting. Lincoln volunteered for the defense. A witness swore that he saw the prisoner strike the fatal blow. It was night, but he swore that the full moon was shining clear, and he saw everything distinctly. The case seemed hopeless, but Lincoln produced an almanac, and showed that at the hour there was no moon. Then he depicted the crime of perjury with such eloquence that the false witness fled the Court House. One who heard the trial says: "It was near night when he concluded, saying: 'If justice was done, before the sun set it would shine upon his client a free man.'"

The Court charged the jury; they retired, and presently returned a verdict—"Not guilty." The prisoner fell into his weeping mother's arms, and then turned to thank Mr. Lincoln, who, looking out at the sun, said: "It is not yet sundown, and you are free."

One of Lincoln's "Hardest Hits."

In Abbott's "History of the Civil War," the following story is told as one of Lincoln's "hardest hits:" "I once knew," said Lincoln, "a sound churchman by the name of Brown, who was a member of a very sober and pious committee having in charge the erection of a bridge over a dangerous and rapid river.   Several architects failed, and at last Brown said he had a friend named Jones, who had built several bridges and undoubtedly could build that one. So Mr. Jones was called in.

"'Can you build this bridge?' inquired the committee.

"'Yes,' replied Jones, 'or any other.   I could build a bridge to the infernal regions, if necessary!'

The committee were shocked, and Brown felt called upon to defend his friend.   'I know Jones so well,' said he, 'and he is so honest a man and so good an architect, that if he states soberly and positively that he can build a bridge to—to——, why, I believe it; but I feel bound to say that I have my doubts about the abutment on the infernal side.'

"So," said Mr. Lincoln, "when politicians told me that the northern and southern wings of the Democracy could be harmonized, why, I believed them, of course; but I always had my doubts about the 'abutment' on the *other* side."

An Incident Connected with Lincoln's Nomination—A Good Temperance Man.

Immediately after Mr. Lincoln's nomination for President at the Chicago Convention, a committee, of which Governor Morgan, of New York, was Chairman, visited him in Springfield, Ill., where he was officially informed of his nomination.

After this ceremony had passed, Mr. Lincoln remarked to the company, that as an appropriate conclusion to an interview so important and interesting as that which had just transpired, he supposed good manners would require that he should treat the committee with something to drink ; and opening a door that led into a room in the **rear,** he called out "Mary! Mary!"   A girl responded to the call, to whom Mr. Lincoln spoke a few words in an under-tone, and, closing the door, returned again to converse with his guests. In a few minutes the maiden entered, bearing a large waiter, containing several glass tumblers, and a large pitcher in the midst, and placed it upon the centre-table. Mr. Lincoln arose, and gravely addressing the company, said : " Gentlemen, we must pledge our mutual healths in the most healthy beverage which God has given to man—it is the only beverage I have ever used or allowed in my family, and I can not conscientiously depart from it on the present occasion—it is pure Adam's ale from the spring ; " and, taking a tumbler, he touched it to his lips, and pledged them his highest respects in a cup of *cold water*. Of course, all his guests were constrained to admire his consistency, and to join in his example.

Gen. Linder's Account of the Lincoln-Shields Duel—Why Lincoln Chose Broadswords as Weapons.

When the famous challenge was sent by General Shields to Mr. Lincoln, it was at once accepted, and by the advice of his especial friend and second, Dr. Merriman, he chose broadswords as the weapons with which to fight. Dr. Merriman being a splendid swordsman trained him in the use of that instrument, which made it almost certain that Shields would be killed or discomfited, for he was a small, short-armed man, while Lincoln was a tall, sinewy, long-armed man, and as stout as Hercules.

They went to Alton, and were to fight on the neck of land between the Missouri and Mississippi Rivers, near their confluence. John J. Hardin, hearing of the contemplated duel, determined to prevent it, and hastened to Alton, with all imaginable celerity, where he fell in with the belligerent parties, and aided by some other friends of both Lincoln and Shields, succeeded in effecting a reconciliation.

After this affair between Lincoln and Shields, I met Lincoln at the Danville court, and in a walk we took together, seeing him make passes with a stick, such as are made in the broadsword exercise, I was induced to ask him why he had selected that weapon with which to fight Shields. He promptly answered in that sharp, ear-splitting voice of his:

" To tell you the truth, Linder, I did not want to kill Shields, and felt sure I could disarm him, having had about a month to learn the broadsword exercise; and furthermore, I didn't want the darned fellow to kill me, which I rather think he would have done if we had selected pistols."

Lincoln's Gratitude—He Volunteers to Defend the Son of an Old Friend Indicted for Murder—How He Was Acquitted.

Jack Armstrong, the leader of the " Clary Grove Boys," with whom Lincoln in early life had a scuffle which "Jack" agreed to call "a drawn battle," in consequence of his own foul play, afterwards became a life-long, warm friend of Mr. Lincoln. Later in life the rising lawyer would stop at Jack's cabin home, and here Mrs. Armstrong, a most womanly person, learned to respect Mr. Lincoln. There was no service to which she did not make her guest abundantly welcome, and he never ceased to feel the tenderest gratitude for her kindness.

At length her husband died, and she became dependent upon her sons. The oldest of these, while in attendance upon a camp-meeting, found himself involved in a melee, which resulted in the death of a young man, and young Armstrong was charged by one of his associates with striking the fatal blow. He was arrested, examined, and imprisoned to await his trial. The public mind was in a blaze of excitement, and interested parties fed the flame. Mr. Lincoln knew nothing of the merits of this case, that is certain. He only knew that his old friend Mrs. Armstrong was in sore trouble; and he sat down at once, and volunteered by letter to defend her son. His first act was to procure the postponement and a change of the place of the trial. There was too much fever in the minds of the immediate public to permit of fair treatment. When the trial came on, the case looked very hopeless to all but Mr. Lincoln, who had assured himself that the young man was not guilty. The evidence on behalf of the state being all in, and looking like a solid and consistent mass of testimony against the prisoner, Mr. Lincoln undertook the task of analyzing and destroying it, which he did in a manner that surprised every one. The principal witness testified that " by the aid of the brightly shining moon, he saw the prisoner inflict the death blow with a slung shot." Mr. Lincoln proved by the almanac that there was no moon shining at the time. The mass of testimony against the prisoner melted away, until "not guilty" was the verdict of every man present in the crowded court-room. There is, of course, no record of the plea made on this occasion, but it is remembered as one in which Mr. Lincoln made an appeal to the sympathies of the jury, which quite surpassed his usual efforts of the kind, and melted all to tears. The jury were out but half an hour, when they returned with their verdict of "not guilty." The widow fainted in the arms of her son, who divided his attention between his services to her and his thanks to his deliverer. And thus the kind woman who cared for the poor young man, and showed herself a mother to him in his need, received the life of a son, saved from a cruel conspiracy, as her reward, from the hand of her grateful beneficiary.

An Honest Lawyer—Some of Lincoln's "Cases" and How He Treated Them.

A sheep-grower on a certain occasion sold a number of sheep at a stipulated average price. When he delivered the animals, he delivered many lambs, or sheep too young to come fairly within the terms of the contract. He was sued for damages by the injured party, and Mr. Lincoln was his attorney. At the trial, the facts as to the character of the sheep delivered were proved, and several witnesses testified as to the usuage by which all under a certain age were regarded as lambs, and of inferior value. Mr. Lincoln, on comprehending the facts, at once changed his line of effort, and confined himself to ascertaining the real number of inferior sheep delivered. On addressing the jury, he said that from the facts proved, they must give a verdict against his client, and he only asked their scrutiny as to the actual damage suffered.

In another case, Mr. Lincoln was conducting a suit against a railroad company. Judgment having been given in his favor, and the court being about to allow the amount claimed by him, deducting a proved and allowed offset, he rose and stated that his opponents had not proved all that was justly due them in offset; and proceeded to state and allow a further sum against his client, which the court allowed in its judgment. His desire for the establishment of exact justice overcame his own selfish love of victory, as well as his partiality for his clients' feelings and interests.

Lincoln's Pungent Retort.

A little incident occurred during a political campaign that illustrated Mr. Lincoln's readiness in turning a political point. He was making a speech at Charleston, Coles County, Illinois, when a voice called out, " Mr. Lincoln, is it true that you entered this state barefoot, driving a yoke of oxen?" Mr. Lincoln paused for full half a minute, as if considering whether he should notice such cruel impertinence, and then said that he thought he could prove the fact by at least a dozen men in the crowd, any one of whom was more respectable than his questioner. But the question seemed to inspire him, and he went on to show what free institutions had done for himself, and to exhibit the evils of slavery to the white man wherever it existed, and asked if it was not natural that he should hate slavery and agitate against it. "Yes," said he, "we will speak for freedom and against slavery, as long as the Constitution of our country guarantees free speech, until everywhere on this wide land the sun shall shine, and the rain shall fall, and the wind shall blow upon no man who goes forth to unrequited toil."

A Revolutionary Pensioner Defended by Lincoln—An Interesting Incident.

An old woman of seventy-five years, the widow of a revolutionary pensioner, came tottering into his law office one day, and, taking a seat, told him that a certain pension agent had charged her the exorbitant fee of two hundred dollars for collecting her claim. Mr. Lincoln was satisfied by her representations that she had been swindled, and finding that she was not a resident of the town, and that she was poor, gave her money, and set about the work of procuring restitution. He immediately entered suit against the agent to recover a portion of his ill-gotten money. The suit was entirely successful, and Mr. Lincoln's address to the jury before which the case was tried is remembered to have been peculiarly touching in its allusions to the poverty of the widow, and the patriotism of the husband she had sacrificed to secure the nation's independence. He had the gratification of paying back to her a hundred dollars, and sending her home rejoicing.

A Thrilling Story—Lincoln Threatens a Twenty Years' Agitation in Illinois.

One afternoon an old negro woman came into the office of Lincoln & Herndon, in Springfield, and told the story of her trouble, to which both lawyers listened. It appeared that she and her offspring were born slaves in Kentucky, and that her owner, one Hinkle, had brought the whole family into Illinois, and given them their freedom. Her son had gone down the Mississippi as a waiter or deck hand, on a steamboat. Arriving at New Orleans, he had imprudently gone ashore, and had been snatched up by the police, in accordance with the law then in force concerning free negroes from other states, and thrown into confinement. Subsequently, he was brought out and tried. Of course he was fined, and, the boat having left, he was sold, or was in immediate danger of being sold, to pay his fine and the expenses. Mr. Lincoln was very much moved, and requested Mr. Herndon to go over to the State House, and inquire of Governor Bissell if there was not something he could do to obtain possession of the negro. Mr. Herndon made the inquiry, and returned with the report that the Governor regretted to say that he had no legal or constitutional right to do anything in the premises. Mr. Lincoln rose to his feet in great excitement, and exclaimed, " By the Almighty, I'll have that negro back soon, or I'll have a twenty years' agitation in Illinois, until the Governor does have a legal and constitutional right to do something in the premises." He was saved from the latter alternative—at least in the direct form which he proposed. The lawyers sent money to a New Orleans correspondent—money of their own—who procured the negro, and returned him to his mother.

Lincoln as a Story Teller—How he always Turned the Story to his advantage—A Practical Example.

One of his modes of getting rid of troublesome friends, as well as troublesome enemies, was by telling a story. He began these tactics early in life, and he grew to be wonderfully adept in them. If a man broached a subject which he did not wish to discuss, he told a story which changed the direction of the conversation. If he was called upon to answer a question, he answered it by telling a story. He had a story for everything—something had occurred at some place where he used to live, that illustrated every possible phase of every possible subject with which he might have connection. His faculty of finding or making a story to match every event in his history, and every event to which he bore any relation, was really marvelous.

That he made, or adapted, some of his stories, there is no question. It is beyond belief that those which entered his mind left it no richer than they came. It is not to be supposed that he spent any time in elaborating them, but by some law of association every event that occurred suggested some story, and, almost by an involuntary process, his mind harmonized their discordant points, and the story was pronounced "pat," because it was made so before it was uttered. Every truth, or combination of truths, seemed immediately to clothe itself in a form of life, where he kept it for reference. His mind was full of stories; and the great facts of his life and history on entering his mind seemed to take up their abode in these stories, and if the garment did not fit them it was so modified that it did.

A good instance of the execution which he sometimes effected with a story, occurred in the legislature. There was a troublesome member from Wabash County, who gloried particularly in being a " strict constructionist." He found something " unconstitutional " in every measure that was brought forward for discussion. He was a member of the Judiciary Committee, and was very apt, after giving every measure a heavy pounding, to advocate its reference to this committee. No amount of sober argument could floor the member from Wabash. At last he came to be considered a man to be silenced, and Mr. Lincoln was resorted to for an expedient by which this object might be accomplished. He soon afterwards honored the draft thus made upon him.

A measure was brought forward in which Mr. Lincoln's constituents were interested, when the member from Wabash rose and discharged all his batteries upon its unconstitutional points. Mr. Lincoln then took the floor, and, with the quizzical expression of features which he could assume at will, and a mirthful twinkle in his gray eyes, said: " Mr. Speaker, the attack of the member from Wabash on the constitutionality of this measure, reminds me of an old friend of mine. He's a peculiar looking old fellow, with shaggy, overhanging eyebrows, and a pair of spectacles under them. (Everybody turned to the member from Wabash, and recognized a personal description.) One morning just after the old man got up, he imagined, on looking out of his door, that he saw rather a lively squirrel on a tree near his house. So he took down his rifle and fired at the squirrel, but the squirrel paid no attention to the shot. He loaded and fired again, and again, until, at the thirteenth shot, he set down his gun impatiently, and said to his boy, who was looking on:

" ' Boy, there's something wrong about this rifle.'

"'Rifle's all right, I know 'tis,' responded the boy, 'but where's your squirrel?'

"'Don't you see him, humped up about half way up the tree?' inquired the old man, peering over his spectacles, and getting mystified.

"'No, I don't,' responded the boy; and then turning and looking into his father's face, he exclaimed, 'I see your squirrel! You 've been firing at a louse on your eyebrow!'"

The story needed neither application nor explanation. The House was in convulsions of laughter; for Mr. Lincoln's skill in telling a story was not inferior to his appreciation of its points and his power of adapting them to the case in hand. It killed off the member from Wabash, who was very careful afterwards not to provoke any allusion to his "eyebrows."

Hon. Newton Bateman's Thrilling Story of Mr. Lincoln—The Great Man Looking to See How the Springfield Preachers Voted—His Surprise, and What Lincoln Said About It.

At the time of the Lincoln nomination, at Chicago, Mr. Newton Bateman, Superintendent of Public Instruction for the State of Illinois, occupied a room adjoining and opening into the Executive Chamber at Springfield. Frequently this door was open during Mr. Lincoln's receptions, and throughout the seven months or more of his occupation, he saw him nearly every day. Often when Mr. Lincoln was tired, he closed the door against all intruders, and called Mr. Bateman into his room for a quiet talk. On one of these occasions, Mr. Lincoln took up a book containing a careful canvass of the city of Springfield, in which he lived, showing the candidate for whom each citizen had declared it his intention to vote in the approaching election. Mr. Lincoln's friends had, doubtless at his own request, placed the result of the canvass in his hands. This was towards the close of October, and only a few days before election. Calling Mr. Bateman to a seat by his side, having previously locked all the doors, he said : 'Let us look over this book; I wish particularly to see how the ministers of Springfield are going to vote.' The leaves were turned, one by one, and as the names were examined Mr. Lincoln frequently asked if this one and that were not a minister, or an elder, or a member of such or such church, and sadly expressed his surprise on receiving an affirmative answer. In that manner they went through the book, and then he closed it and sat silently for some minutes regarding a memorandum in pencil which lay before him. At length he turned to Mr. Bateman, with a face full of sadness, and said : 'Here are twenty-three ministers, of different denominations, and all of them are against me but three, and here are a great many prominent members of the churches, a very large majority are against me. Mr. Bateman, I am not a Christian,—God knows I would be one,— but I have carefully read the Bible, and I do not so understand this book;' and he drew forth a pocket New Testament. 'These men well know,' he continued, 'that I am for freedom in the Territories, freedom everywhere as free as the Constitution and the laws will permit, and that my opponents are for slavery. They *know* this, and yet, with this book in their hands, in the light of which human bondage can not live a moment, they are going to vote against me; I do not understand it at all.'

"Here Mr. Lincoln paused—paused for long minutes— his features surcharged with emotion. Then he rose and walked up and down the reception-room in the effort to retain or regain his self-possession. Stopping at last, he said, with a trembling voice and cheeks wet with tears: 'I know there is a God, and that he hates injustice and slavery. I see the storm coming, and I know that His hand is in it. If He has a place and work for me, and I think He has, I believe I am ready. I am nothing, but Truth is everything. I know I am right, because I know that liberty is right, for Christ teaches it, and Christ is God. I have told them that a house divided against itself can not stand; and Christ and Reason say the same; and they will find it so.'

" 'Douglas don't care whether slavery is voted up or down, but God cares, and humanity cares, and I care; and with God's help I shall not fail. I may not see the end; but it will come, and I shall be vindicated; and these men will find that they have not read their Bible right.'

" Much of this was uttered as if he was speaking to himself, and with a sad, earnest solemnity of manner impossi-ble to be described. After a pause, he resumed: 'Doesn't it appear strange that men can ignore the moral aspect of this contest? A revelation could not make it plainer to me that slavery or the Government must be destroyed. The future would be something awful, as I look at it, but for this rock on which I stand,' (alluding to the Testament which he still held in his hand,) ' especially with the knowl-edge of how these ministers are going to vote. It seems as if God had borne with this thing (slavery) until the very teachers of religion had come to defend it from the Bible, and to claim for it a divine character and sanction; and now the cup of iniquity is full, and the vials of wrath will be poured out.' After this the conversation was continued for a long time. Everything he said was of a peculiarly deep, tender, and religious tone, and all was tinged with a touching melancholy. He repeatedly referred to his con-viction that the day of wrath was at hand, and that he was to be an actor in the terrible struggle which would issue in the overthrow of slavery, though he might not live to see the end.

"After further reference to a belief in Divine Providence and the fact of God in history, the conversation turned upon prayer. He freely stated his belief in the duty, privilege, and efficacy of prayer, and intimated, in no unmistakable terms, that he had sought in that way the Divine guidance and favor. The effect of this conversation upon the mind of Mr. Bateman, a Christian gentleman whom Mr. Lincoln profoundly respected, was to convince him that Mr. Lincoln had, in his quiet way, found a path to the Christian stand-point — that he had found God, and rested on the eternal truth of God. As the two men were about to separate, Mr. Bateman remarked : ' I have not supposed that you were accustomed to think so much upon this class of subjects ; certainly your friends generally are ignorant of the senti-ments you have expressed to me.' He replied quickly : ' I know they are, but I think more on these subjects than upon all others, and I have done so for years; and I am willing you should know it.' "

WHEN his clients had practiced gross deception upon him, Mr. Lincoln forsook their cases in mid-passage; and he al-ways refused to accept fees of those whom he advised not to prosecute. On one occasion, while engaged upon an important case, he discovered that he was on the wrong side. His associate in the case was immediately informed that he (Lincoln) would not make the plea. The associate made it, and the case, much to the surprise of Lincoln, was decided for his client. Perfectly convinced that his client was wrong, he would not receive one cent of the fee of nine hundred dollars which he paid. It is not wonderful that one who knew him well spoke of him as " perversely honest."

[UNITED STATES CAPITOL.]

WHITE-HOUSE INCIDENTS.

Trying the "Greens" on Jake—A Serious Experiment.

A deputation of bankers were one day introduced to the President by the Secretary of the Treasury. One of the party, Mr. P—— of Chelsea, Mass., took occasion to refer to the severity of the tax laid by Congress upon the State Banks.

"Now," said Mr. Lincoln, "that reminds me of a circumstance that took place in a neighborhood where I lived when I was a boy. In the spring of the year the farmers were very fond of the dish which they called greens, though the fashionable name for it now-a-days is spinach, I believe. One day after dinner, a large family were taken very ill. The doctor was called in, who attributed it to the greens, of which all had freely partaken. Living in the family was a half-witted boy named Jake. On a subsequent occasion, when greens had been gathered for dinner, the head of the house said : ' Now, boys, before running any further risk in this thing, we will first try them on Jake. If he stands it, we are all right.' And just so, I suppose," said Mr. Lincoln, " Congress thought it would try this tax on the State Banks ! "

A Little Story which Lincoln told the Preachers.

A year or more before Mr. Lincoln's death, a delegation of clergymen waited upon him in reference to the appointment of the army chaplains. The delegation consisted of a Presbyterian, a Baptist, and an Episcopal clergyman.

They stated that the character of many of the chaplains was notoriously bad, and they had come to urge upon the President the necessity of more discretion in these appointments.

"But, gentlemen," said the President, "that is a matter which the Government has nothing to do with; the chaplains are chosen by the regiments."

Not satisfied with this, the clergymen pressed, in turn, a change in the system. Mr. Lincoln heard them through without remark, and then said, "Without any disrespect, gentlemen, I will tell you a 'little story.'

"Once, in Springfield, I was going off on a short journey, and reached the depot a little ahead of time. Leaning against the fence just outside the depot was a little darkey boy, whom I knew, named 'Dick,' busily digging with his toe in a mud-puddle. As I came up, I said, 'Dick, what are you about?'

"'Making a *church*,' said he.

"'A church?' said I; 'what do you mean?'

"'Why, yes,' said Dick, pointing with his toe, 'don't you see? there is the shape of it; there's the steps and front-door—here the pews, where the folks set—and there's the pulpit.'

"'Yes, I see,' said I, 'but why don't you make a minister?'

"'Laws,' answered Dick, with a grin, 'I hain't got *mud* enough!'"

How Lincoln Stood up for the Word " Sugar-Coated."

Mr. Defrees, the government printer, states, that, when one of the President's messages was being printed, he was a good deal disturbed by the use of the term "sugar-coated," and finally went to Mr. Lincoln about it. Their relations to each other being of the most intimate character, he told the President frankly, that he ought to remember that a message to Congress was a different affair from a speech at a mass meeting in Illinois ; that the messages became a part of history, and should be written accordingly.

"What is the matter now ?" inquired the President.

"Why," said Mr. Defrees, "you have used an undignified expression in the message ;" and then, reading the paragraph aloud, he added, " I would alter the structure of that, if I were you."

" Defrees," replied Mr. Lincoln, " that word expresses precisely my idea, and I am not going to change it. The time will never come in this country when the people won't know exactly what *sugar-coated* means ! "

On a subsequent occasion, Mr. Defrees states that a certain sentence of another message was very awkwardly constructed. Calling the President's attention to in the proof-copy, the latter acknowledged the force of the objection raised, and said, " Go home, Defrees, and see if you can better it."

The next day Mr. Defrees took in to him his amendment. Mr. Lincoln met him by saying : " Seward found the same fault that you did, and he has been rewriting the paragraph, also." Then, reading Mr. Defrees' version, he said, " I believe you have beaten Seward; but, ' I jings,' I think I can beat you both." Then, taking up his pen, he wrote the sentence as it was finally printed.

Lincoln's Advice to a Prominent Bachelor.

Upon the bethrothal of the Prince of Wales to the Princess Alexandra, Queen Victoria sent a letter to each of the European sovereigns, and also to President Lincoln, announcing the fact. Lord Lyons, her ambassador at Washington,—a "bachelor," by the way,—requested an audience of Mr. Lincoln, that he might present this important document in person. At the time appointed he was received at the White House, in company with Mr. Seward.

"May it please your Excellency," said Lord Lyons, "I hold in my hand an autograph letter from my royal mistress, Queen Victoria, which I have been commanded to present to your Excellency. In it she informs your Excellency, that her son, his Royal Highness the Prince of Wales, is about to contract a matrimonial alliance with her Royal Highness the Princess Alexandra of Denmark."

After continuing in this strain for a few minutes, Lord Lyons tendered the letter to the President and awaited his reply. It was short, simple, and expressive, and consisted simply of the words:

"Lord Lyons, *go thou and do likewise.*"

It is doubtful if an English ambassador was ever addressed in this manner before, and it would be interesting to learn what success he met with in putting the reply in diplomatic language when he reported it to her Majesty.

Mr. Lincoln and the Bashful Boys—He Tells a Story of Daniel Webster.

The President and a friend were standing upon the threshold of the door under the portico of the White House, awaiting the coachman, when a letter was put into his hand. While he was reading this, people were passing, as is customary, up and down the promenade, which leads through the grounds to the War Department, crossing, of course, the portico. Attention was attracted to an approaching party, apparently a countryman, plainly dressed, with his wife and two little boys, who had evidently been straying about, looking at the places of public interest in the city. As they reached the portico, the father, who was in advance, caught sight of the tall figure of Mr. Lincoln, absorbed in his letter. His wife and the little boys were ascending the steps.

The man stopped suddenly, put out his hand with a "hush" to his family, and, after a moment's gaze, he bent down and whispered to them, " There is the President!" Then leaving them, he slowly made a half circuit around Mr. Lincoln, watching him intently all the while.

At this point, having finished his letter, the President turned and said: " Well, we will not wait any longer for the carriage; it won't hurt you and me to walk down."

The countryman here approached very diffidently, and asked if he might be allowed to take the President by the hand; after which, " Would he extend the same privilege to his wife and little boys?"

Mr. Lincoln, good-naturedly, approached the latter, who had remained where they were stopped, and, reaching down, said a kind word to the bashful little fellows, who shrank close up to their mother, and did not reply. This simple act filled the father's cup full.

" The Lord is with you, Mr. President," he said, reverently; and then, hesitating a moment, he added, with strong emphasis, " *and the people, too, sir; and the people, too!*"

A few moments later Mr. Lincoln remarked to his friend: "Great men have various estimates. When Daniel Webster made his tour through the West years ago, he visited Springfield among other places, where great preparations had been made to receive him. As the procession was going through the town, a barefooted little darkey boy pulled the sleeve of a man named T., and asked :

" ' What the folks were all doing down the street?'

" ' Why, Jack,' was the reply, 'the biggest man in the world is coming.'

" Now, there lived in Springfield a man by the name of G.—a very corpulent man. Jack darted off down the street, but presently returned, with a very disappointed air.

" ' Well, did you see him?' inquired T.

" ' Yees,' returned Jack; ' but laws—he ain't *half as big as old G.* ' "

An Irish Soldier Who Wanted Something Stronger than Soda-Water.

Upon Mr. Lincoln's return to Washington, after the capture of Richmond, a member of the Cabinet asked him if it would be proper to permit Jacob Thompson to slip through Maine in disguise, and embark from Portland. The President, as usual, was disposed to be merciful, and to permit the arch-rebel to pass unmolested, but the Secretary urged that he should be arrested as a traitor. "By permitting him to escape the penalties of treason," persistently remarked the Secretary, "you sanction it." "Well," replied Mr. Lincoln, "let me tell you a story.

" There was an Irish soldier here last Summer, who wanted something to drink stronger than water, and stopped at a drug-shop, where he espied a soda-fountain.

" ' Mr. Doctor,' said he, ' give me, plase, a glass of soda-wather, an' if yees can put in a few drops of whisky unbeknown to any one, I'll be obleeged.'

" Now," said Mr. Lincoln, "if Jake Thompson is permitted to go through Maine unbeknown to any one, what's the harm? So don't have him arrested."

Looking Out for Breakers—How the President Illustrated It.

In a time of despondency, some visitors were telling the President of the " breakers " so often seen ahead—" this time surely coming." " That," said he, " suggests the story of the school-boy, who never could pronounce the names 'Shadrach,' 'Meshach,' and 'Abednego.' He had been repeatedly whipped for it without effect. Sometime afterwards he saw the names in the regular lesson for the day. Putting his finger upon the place, he turned to his next neighbor, an older boy, and whispered, ' Here comes those *" tormented Hebrews" again!'* "

Work Enough for Twenty Presidents Illustrated by a Story About Jack Chase.

A farmer from one of the border counties went to the President on a certain occasion with the complaint that the Union soldiers in passing his farm had helped themselves not only to hay but to his horse; and he hoped the proper officer would be required to consider his claim immediately.

" Why, my good sir," replied Mr. Lincoln, " if I should attempt to consider every such individual case, I should find work enough for twenty Presidents !

" In my early days, I knew one Jack Chase, who was a lumberman on the Illinois, and, when steady and sober, the best raftsman on the river. It was quite a trick twenty-five years ago to take the logs over the rapids, but he was skillful with a raft, and always kept her straight in the channel. Finally a steamer was put on, and Jack—he's dead now, poor fellow !—was made captain of her. He always used to take the wheel going through the rapids. One day, when the boat was plunging and wallowing along the boiling current, and Jack's utmost vigilance was being exercised to keep her in the narrow channel, a boy pulled his coat-tail and hailed him with: 'Say, Mister Captain! I wish you would just stop your boat a minute—I've lost my apple overboard!'"

Philosophy of Canes—The Kind Lincoln Made and Carried When a Boy.

A gentleman calling at the White House one evening carried a cane, which, in the course of conversation, attracted the President's attention. Taking it in his hand, he said: " I always used a cane when I was a boy. It was a freak of mine. My favorite one was a knotted beech stick, and I carved the head myself. There's a mighty amount of character in sticks. Don't you think so? You have seen these fishing-poles that fit into a cane? Well, that was an old idea of mine. Dogwood clubs were favorite ones with the boys. I suppose they use them yet. Hickory is too heavy, unless you get it from a young sapling. Have you ever noticed how a stick in one's hand will change his appearance? Old women and witches wouldn't look so without sticks. Meg Merrilies understands that."

Stories Illustrating Lincoln's Memory.

Mr. Lincoln's memory was very remarkable. At one of the afternoon receptions at the White House, a stranger shook hands with him, and, as he did so, remarked, casually, that he was elected to Congress about the time Mr. Lincoln's term as representative expired, which happened many years before.

"Yes," said the President, "you are from ——," mentioning the state. " I remember reading of your election in a newspaper one morning on a steamboat going down to Mount Vernon."

At another time a gentleman addressed him, saying, " I presume, Mr. President, that you have forgotten me?"

" No," was the prompt reply; " your name is Flood. I saw you last, twelve years ago, at ——," naming the place and the occasion. " I am glad to see," he continued, " that the *Flood* flows on."

Subsequent to his re-election a deputation of bankers from various sections were introduced one day by the Secretary of the Treasury. After a few moments of general conversation, Mr. Lincoln turned to one of them, and said: " Your district did not give me so strong a vote at the last election as it did in 1860."

" I think, sir, that you must be mistaken," replied the banker. " I have the impression that your majority was considerably increased at the last election."

" No," rejoined the President, "you fell off about six hundred votes." Then taking down from the book-case the official canvass of 1860 and 1864, he referred to the vote of the district named, and proved to be quite right in his assertion.

Common Sense.

The Hon. Mr. Hubbard, of Connecticut, once called upon the President in reference to a newly invented gun, concerning which a committee had been appointed to make a report.

The "report" was sent for, and when it came in was found to be of the most voluminous description. Mr. Lincoln glanced at it, and said: " I should want a new lease of life to read this through!" Throwing it down upon the table, he added: " Why can't a committee of this kind occasionally exhibit a grain of common sense? If I send a man to buy a horse for me, I expect him to tell me his *points*—not how many *hairs* there are in his tail.

Lincoln's Confab with a Committee on "Grant's Whisky."

Just previous to the fall of Vicksburg, a self-constituted committee, solicitous for the *morale* of our armies, took it upon themselves to visit the President and urge the removal of General Grant.

In some surprise Mr. Lincoln inquired, " For what reason?"

" Why," replied the spokesman, " he drinks too much whisky."

" Ah!" rejoined Mr. Lincoln, dropping his lower lip. "By the way, gentlemen, can either of you tell me where General Grant procures his whisky? because, if I can find out, I will send every general in the field *a barrel of it!*"

A "Pretty Tolerable Respectable Sort of a Clergyman."

Some one was discussing, in the presence of Mr. Lincoln, the character of a time-serving Washington clergyman. Said Mr. Lincoln to his visitor:

" I think you are rather hard upon Mr. ——. He reminds me of a man in Illinois, who was tried for passing a counterfeit bill. It was in evidence that before passing it he had taken it to the cashier of a bank and asked his opinion of the bill, and he received a very prompt reply that it was a counterfeit. His lawyer, who had heard the evidence to be brought against his client, asked him, just before going into court, ' Did you take the bill to the cashier of the bank and ask him if it was good?'

" ' I did,' was the reply.

" ' Well, what was the reply of the cashier?'

" The rascal was in a corner, but he got out of it in this fashion: ' He said it was a pretty tolerable, respectable sort of a bill.' " Mr. Lincoln thought the clergyman was " a pretty tolerable, respectable sort of a clergyman."

WHITE PIGEON CHURCH.

The unpretentious edifice where Abraham Lincoln attended Divine Service in early life.

How Lincoln Opened the Eyes of an Inquisitive Visitor.

Mr. Lincoln sometimes had a very effective way of dealing with men who troubled him with questions. A visitor once asked him how many men the Rebels had in the field.

The President replied, very seriously, "*Twelve hundred thousand, according to the best authority.*"

The interrogator blanched in the face, and ejaculated, "*Good Heavens!*"

"Yes, sir, twelve hundred thousand—no doubt of it. You see, all of our generals, when they get whipped, say the enemy outnumbers them from three or five to one, and I must believe them. We have four hundred thousand men in the field, and three times four make twelve. Don't you see it?"

Minnehaha and Minneboohoo!

Some gentlemen fresh from a Western tour, during a call at the White House, referred in the course of conversation to a body of water in Nebraska, which bore an Indian name signifying "weeping water." Mr. Lincoln instantly responded: "As 'laughing water,' according to Longfellow, is 'Minnehaha,' this evidently should be 'Minneboohoo.'"

Meeting of President Lincoln and the Artist, Carpenter.

F. B. Carpenter, the celebrated artist and author of the well-known painting of Lincoln and his Cabinet issuing the Emancipation Proclamation, describes his first meeting with the President, as follows:

"Two o'clock found me one of the throng pressing toward the center of attraction, the 'blue' room. From the threshold of the 'crimson' parlor as I passed, I had a glimpse of the gaunt figure of Mr. Lincoln in the distance, haggard-looking, dressed in black, relieved only by the prescribed white gloves; standing, it seemed to me, solitary and alone, though surrounded by the crowd, bending low now and then in the process of hand-shaking, and responding half abstractedly to the well-meant greetings of the miscellaneous assemblage.

"Never shall I forget the electric thrill which went through my whole being at this instant. I seemed to see lines radiating from every part of the globe, converging to a focus at the point where that plain, awkward-looking man stood, and to hear in spirit a million prayers, ' as the sound of many waters,' ascending in his behalf. Mingled with supplication I could discern a clear symphony of triumph and blessing, swelling with an ever-increasing volume. It was the voice of those who had been bondmen and bond-women, and the grand diapason swept up from the coming ages.

"It was soon my privilege, in the regular succession, to take that honored hand. Accompanying the act, my name and profession were announced to him in a low tone by one of the assistant private secretaries, who stood by his side. Retaining my hand, he looked at me inquiringly for an instant, and said, ' Oh, yes; I know; this is the painter.' Then straightening himself to his full height, with a twinkle of the eye, he added, playfully, " Do you think, Mr. C——, that you can make a handsome picture of *me?*" emphasizing strongly the last word. Somewhat confused at this point-blank shot, uttered in a tone so loud as to attract the attention of those in immediate proximity, I made a random reply, and took the occasion to ask if I could see him in his study at the close of the reception. To this he responded in the peculiar vernacular of the West, ' I reckon,' resuming meanwhile the mechanical and traditional exercise of the hand which no President has ever yet been able to avoid, and which, severe as is the ordeal, is likely to attach to the position so long as the Republic endures."

An Apt Illustration.

At the White House one day some gentlemen were present from the West, excited and troubled about the commissions or omissions of the Administration. The President heard them patiently, and then replied: " Gentlemen, suppose all the property you were worth was in gold, and you had put it in the hands of Blondin to carry across the Niagara River on a rope, would you shake the cable, or keep shouting out to him, 'Blondin, stand up a little straighter—Blondin, stoop a little more—go a little faster—lean a little more to the north—lean a little more to the south?' No! you would hold your breath as well as your tongue, and keep your hands off until he was safe over. The Government is carrying an immense weight. Untold treasures are in their hands. They are doing the very best they can. Don't badger them. Keep silence, and we'll get you safe across."

More Light and Less Noise.

An editorial, in a New York journal, opposing Lincoln's re-nomination, is said to have called out from him the following story: A traveler on the frontier found himself out of his reckoning one night in a most inhospitable region. A terrific thunder-storm came up, to add to his trouble. He floundered along until his horse at length gave out. The lightning afforded him the only clew to his way, but the peals of thunder were frightful. One bolt, which seemed to crash the earth beneath him, brought him to his knees.

By no means a praying man, his petition was short and to the point—" O Lord, if it is all the same to you, give us a little *more light and a little less noise!*"

How Lincoln " Browsed" Around.

A party of gentlemen, among whom was a doctor of divinity of much dignity of manner, calling at the White House one day, was informed by the porter that the President was at dinner, but that he would present their cards. The doctor demurred at this, saying that he would call again. "Edward" assured them that he thought it would make no difference, and went in with the cards. In a few minutes the President walked into the room, with a kindly salutation, and a request that the friends would take seats. The doctor expressed his regret that their visit was so ill-timed, and that his Excellency was disturbed while at dinner. "Oh! no consequence at all," said Mr. Lincoln, good-naturedly. "Mrs. Lincoln is absent at present, and when she is away, I generally '*browse*' around."

Lincoln Cutting Red Tape.

"Upon entering the President's office one afternoon," says a Washington correspondent, "I found Mr. Lincoln busily counting greenbacks.

"'This, sir,' said he, 'is something out of my usual line; but a President of the United States has a multiplicity of duties not specified in the Constitution or acts of Congress. This is one of them. This money belongs to a poor negro who is a porter in the Treasury Department, at present very bad with the small-pox. He is now in hospital, and could not draw his pay because he could not sign his name. I have been at considerable trouble to overcome the difficulty and get it for him, and have at length succeeded in *cutting red tape*, as you newspaper men say. I am now dividing the money and putting by a portion labelled, in an envelope, with my own hands, according to his wish ; ' and he proceeded to indorse the package very carefully."

No one witnessing the transaction could fail to appreciate the goodness of heart which prompted the President of the United States to turn aside for a time from his weighty cares to succor one of the humblest of his fellow-creatures in sickness and sorrow.

One of Lincoln's Drolleries.

Concerning a drollery of President Lincoln, this story is told :

" During the Rebellion an Austrian Count applied to President Lincoln for a position in the army. Being introduced by the Austrian Minister, he needed, of course, no further recommendation ; but, as if fearing that his importance might not be duly appreciated, he proceeded to explain that he was a Count ; that his family were ancient and highly respectable; when Lincoln, with a merry twinkle in his eye, tapping the aristocratic lover of titles on the shoulder, in a fatherly way, as if the man had confessed to some wrong, interrupted in a soothing tone, 'Never mind; you shall be treated with just as much consideration for all that ?' "

Anecdote Showing the Methods by which Lincoln and Stanton Dismissed Applicants for Office.

A gentleman states in a Chicago journal: In the Winter of 1864, after serving three years in the Union army, and being honorably discharged, I made application for the post sutlership at Point Lookout. My father being interested, we made application to Mr. Stanton, then Secretary of War. We obtained an audience, and was ushered into the presence of the most pompous man I ever met. As I entered he waved his hand for me to stop at a given distance from him, and then put these questions, viz.:

"Did you serve three years in the army?"

"I did, sir."

"Were you honorably discharged?"

"I was, sir?"

"Let me see your discharge?"

I gave it to him. He looked it over, and then said: "Were you ever wounded?"

I told him yes, at the battle of Williamsburg, May 5, 1861.

He then said: "I think we can give this position to a soldier who has lost an arm or leg, he being more deserving," and he then said that I looked hearty and healthy enough to serve three years more. He would not give me a chance to argue my case. The audience was at an end. He waved his hand to me. I was then dismissed from the august presence of the Honorable Secretary of War.

My father was waiting for me in the hallway, who saw by my countenance that I was not successful. I said to my father, "Let us go over to Mr. Lincoln; he may give us more satisfaction." He said it would do no good, but we went over. Mr. Lincoln's reception room was full of ladies and gentlemen when we entered, and the scene was one I shall never forget. On her knees was a woman in the agonies of despair, with tears rolling down her cheeks, imploring for the life of her son, who had deserted and had been condemned to be shot. I heard Mr. Lincoln say: "Madam, do not act this way, it is agony to me; I would pardon your son if it was in my power, but there must be an example made, or I will have no army."

At this speech the woman fainted. Lincoln motioned to his attendant, who picked the woman up and carried her out. All in the room were in tears.

But, now changing the scene from the sublime to the ridiculous, the next applicant for favor was a big, buxom Irish woman, who stood before the President with arms akimbo, saying, " Mr. Lincoln, can't I sell apples on the railroad?" Lincoln said: " Certainly, madam; you can sell all you wish." But she said, " You must give me a pass or the soldiers will not let me." Lincoln then wrote a few lines and gave it to her, who said, " Thank you, sir; God bless, you." This shows how quick and clear were all this man's decisions.

I stood and watched him for two hours, and he dismissed each case as quickly as the above, with satisfaction to all.

My turn soon came. Lincoln spoke to my father, and said, " Now, gentlemen, be pleased to be as quick as possible with your business, as it is growing late." My father then stepped up to Lincoln and introduced me to him. Lincoln then said, " Take a seat, gentlemen, and state your business as quick as possible." There was but one chair by Lincoln, so he motioned to my father to sit, while I stood. My father stated the business to him as stated above. He then said, " Have you seen Mr. Stanton?" We told him yes, that he had refused. He (Mr. Lincoln) then said: "Gentlemen, this is Mr. Stanton's business; I can not interfere with him; he attends to all these matters, and I am sorry I can not help you."

He saw that we were disappointed, and did his best to revive our spirits. He succeeded well with my father, who was a Lincoln man, and who was a staunch Republican.

Mr. Lincoln then said: " Now, gentlemen, I will tell you what it is; I have thousands of applications like this every day, but we can not satisfy all for this reason, that these positions are like office-seekers, there are too many *pigs for the tits.*"

The ladies who were listening to the conversation placed their handkerchiefs to their faces and turned away. But the joke of Old Abe put us all in a good humor. We then left the presence of the greatest and most just man who ever lived to fill the Presidential chair.

An Instance Where the President's Mind Wandered.

An amusing, yet touching instance of the President's pre-occupation of mind, occurred at one of his levees, when he was shaking hands with a host of visitors passing him in a continuous stream. An intimate acquaintance received the usual conventional hand-shake and salutation, but perceiving that he was not recognized, kept his ground instead of moving on, and spoke again; when the President, roused to a dim consciousness that something unusual had happened, perceived who stood before him, and seizing his friend's hand, shook it again heartily, saying, " How do you do? How do you do? Excuse me for not noticing you. I was thinking of a man down South." He afterward privately acknowledged that the " man down South " was Sherman, then on his march to the sea.

Lincoln and the Preacher.

An officer of the Government called one day at the White House, and introduced a clerical friend. "Mr. President," said he, "allow me to present to you my friend, the Rev. Mr. F., of ——. He has expressed a desire to see you and have some conversation with you, and I am happy to be the means of introducing him."

The President shook hands with Mr. F., and desiring

him to be seated took a seat himself. Then, his countenance having assumed an air of patient waiting, he said: "I am now ready to hear what you have to say." "Oh, bless you, sir," said Mr. F., "I have nothing special to say; I merely called to pay my respects to you, and, as one of the million, to assure you of my hearty sympathy and support."

"My dear sir," said the President, rising promptly, his face showing instant relief, and with both hands grasping that of his visitor, "I am very glad to see you, indeed. *I thought you had come to preach to me!*"

A Home Incident—Lincoln and Little " Tad."

The day after the review of Burnside's division some photographers, says Mr. Carpenter, came up to the White House to make some stereoscopic studies for me of the President's office. They requested a dark closet, in which to develop the pictures; and without a thought that I was infringing upon anybody's rights, I took them to an unoccupied room of which little " Tad " had taken possession a few days before, and with the aid of a couple of the servants, had fitted up as a miniature theatre, with stage, curtains, orchestra, stalls, parquette, and all. Knowing that the use required would interfere with none of his arrangements, I led the way to this apartment.

Everything went on well, and one or two pictures had been taken, when suddenly there was an uproar. The operator came back to the office, and said that " Tad " had taken great offence at the occupation of his room without his consent, and had locked the door, refusing all admission. The chemicals had been taken inside, and there was no way of getting at them, he having carried off the key. In the midst of this conversation, " Tad " burst in, in a fearful passion. He laid all the blame upon me—said that I had no right to use his room, and the men should not go in even to get their things. He had locked the door, and they should not go there again—" they had no business in his room !"

Mr. Lincoln was sitting for a photograph, and was still in the chair. He said, very mildly, " Tad, go and unlock the door." Tad went off muttering into his mother's room, refusing to obey. I followed him into the passage, but no coaxing would pacify him. Upon my return to the President, I found him still sitting patiently in the chair, from which he had not risen. He said: " Has not the boy opened the door?" I replied that we could do nothing with him—he had gone off in a great pet. Mr. Lincoln's lips came together firmly, and then, suddenly rising, he strode across the passage with the air of one bent on punishment, and disappeared in the domestic apartments. Directly he returned with the key to the theatre, which he unlocked himself. " There," said he, " go ahead, it is all right now." He then went back to his office, followed by myself, and resumed his seat. " Tad," said he, half apologetically, " is a peculiar child. He was violently excited when I went to him. I said, ' Tad, do you know you are making your father a great deal of trouble?' He burst into tears, instantly giving me up the key."

A Touching Incident — Lincoln Mourning for His Lost Son is Comforted by Rev. Dr. Vinton.

After the funeral of his son, William Wallace Lincoln, in February, 1862, the President resumed his official duties, but mechanically, and with a terrible weight at his heart. The following Thursday he gave way to his feelings, and shut himself from all society. The second Thursday it was the same; he would see no one, and seemed a prey to the deepest melancholy. About this time the Rev. Francis Vinton, of Trinity Church, New York, had occasion to spend a few days in Washington. An acquaintance of Mrs. Lincoln and of her sister, Mrs. Edwards, of Springfield, he was requested by them to come up and see the President. The setting apart of Thursday for the indulgence of his grief had gone on for several weeks, and Mrs. Lincoln began to be seriously alarmed for the health of her husband, of which fact Dr. Vinton was apprised.

Mr. Lincoln received him in the parlor, and an opportunity was soon embraced by the clergyman to chide him for showing so rebellious a disposition to the decrees of Providence. He told him plainly that the indulgence of such feelings, though natural, was sinful. It was unworthy one who believed in the Christian religion. He had duties to the living, greater than those of any other man, as the chosen father, and leader of the people, and he was unfitting himself for his responsibilities by thus giving way to his grief. To mourn the departed as *lost* belonged to heathenism—not to Christianity. " Your son," said Dr. Vinton, " is *alive*, in Paradise. Do you remember that passage in the Gospels: ' God is not the God of the *dead* but of the living, for *all* live unto Him?' "

The President had listened as one in a stupor, until his ear caught he words, " Your son is alive." Starting from the sofa, he exclaimed, " Alive! *alive!* Surely you mock me."

" No, sir, believe me," replied Dr. Vinton; " it is a most comforting doctrine of the Church, founded upon the words of Christ Himself."

Mr. Lincoln looked at him a moment, and then, stepping forward, he threw his arm around the clergyman's neck, and, laying his head upon his breast, sobbed aloud, " *Alive? alive?*" he repeated.

"My dear sir," said Dr. Vinton, greatly moved, as he twined his own arm around the weeping father, "believe this, for it is God's most precious truth. Seek not your son among the dead; he is not there; he lives to-day in Paradise! Think of the full import of the words I have quoted. The Sadducees, when they questioned Jesus, had no other conception than that Abraham, Isaac, and Jacob were dead and buried. Mark the reply: 'Now that the dead *are* raised, even Moses showed at the bush when he called the Lord the God of Abraham, the God of Isaac, and the God of Jacob. For He is not the God of the dead, but of the living, *for all live unto Him!*' Did not the aged patriarch mourn his sons as dead?—'Joseph is not, and Simeon is not, and ye will take Benjamin, also.' But Joseph and Simeon were both living, though he believed it not. Indeed, Joseph being taken from him, was the eventual means of the preservation of the whole family. And so God has called your son into His upper kingdom—a king-dom and an existence as real, more real, than your own. It may be that he, too, like Joseph, has gone, in God's good providence, to be the salvation of *his* father's household. It is a part of the Lord's plan for the ultimate happiness of you and yours. Doubt it not. I have a sermon," con-tinued Dr. Vinton, "upon this subject, which I think might interest you."

Mr. Lincoln begged him to send it at an early day—thanking him repeatedly for his cheering and hopeful words. The sermon was sent, and read over and over by the President, who caused a copy to be made for his own private use before it was returned.

Lincoln Wipes the Tears from His Eyes and Tells a Story.

A. W. Clark, member of Congress from Watertown, New York, relates the following interesting story: During the war a constituent came to me and stated that one of his sons was killed in a battle, and another died at Andersonville, while the third and only remaining son was sick at Harper's Ferry.

These disasters had such effect on his wife that she had become insane. He wanted to get this last and sick son discharged, and take him home, hoping it would restore his wife to reason. I went with him to President Lincoln and related the facts as well as I could, the father sitting by and weeping. The President, much affected, asked for the papers and wrote across them, "Discharge this man."

Then, wiping the tear from his cheek, he turned to the man at the door, and said "Bring in that man, rather as if he felt bored, which caused me to ask why it was so.

He replied that it was a writing-master who had spent a long time in copying his Emancipation Proclamation, had ornamented it with flourishes, and which made him think of an Irishman who said it took him an hour to catch his old horse, and when he had caught him he was not worth a darn!

Comments of Mr. Lincoln on the Emancipation Proclamation — What He Told Mr. Colfax.

The final proclamation was signed on New Year's Day, 1863. The President remarked to Mr. Colfax, the same evening, that the signature appeared somewhat tremulous and uneven. "Not," said he, "because of any uncertainty or hesitation on my part; but it was just after the public reception, and three hours' hand-shaking is not calculated to improve a man's chirography." Then, changing his tone, he added: "The South had fair warning, that if they did not return to their duty, I should strike at this pillar of their strength. The promise must now be kept, and I shall never recall one word."

Lincoln Arguing Against the Emancipation Proclamation That He May Learn all about It.

When Lincoln's judgment, which acted slowly, but which was almost as immovable as the eternal hills when settled, was grasping some subject of importance, the arguments against his own desires seemed uppermost in his mind, and, in conversing upon it, he would present those arguments to see if they could be rebutted.

This is illustrated by the interview between himself and the Chicago delegation of clergymen, appointed to urge upon him the issue of a Proclamation of Emancipation, which occurred September 13, 1862, more than a month after he had declared to the Cabinet his established purpose to take this step.

He said to this committee: "I do not want to issue a document that the whole world will see must necessarily be inoperative, like the Pope's bull against the comet!" After drawing out their views ipon the subject, he concluded the interview with those memorable words:

"Do not misunderstand me, because I have mentioned these objections. They indicate the difficulties which have thus far prevented my action in some such way as you desire. I have not decided against a proclamation of liberty to the slaves, but hold the matter under advisement. And I can assure you that the subject is on my mind, by day and night, more than any other. Whatever shall appear to be God's will, I will do! I trust that, in the freedom with which I have canvassed your views, I have not in any respect injured your feelings."

Lincoln's Laugh—What Hon. I. N. Arnold Said About It.

Mr. Lincoln's "laugh" stood by itself. The "neigh" of a wild horse on his native prairie is not more undisguised and hearty. A group of gentlemen, among whom was his old Springfield friend and associate, Hon. Isaac N. Arnold, were one day conversing in the passage near his office, while awaiting admission. A congressional delegation had preceded them, and presently an unmistakable voice was heard through the partition, in a burst of mirth. Mr. Arnold remarked, as the sound died away: *"That laugh has been the President's life-preserver!"*

Lincoln and the Newspapers.

On a certain occasion, the President was induced by a committee of gentlemen to examine a newly-invented "repeating" gun, the peculiarity of which was, that it prevented the escape of gas. After due inspection, he said: "Well, I believe this really does what it is represented to do. Now, have any of you heard of any machine or invention for preventing the escape of 'gas' from newspaper establishments?"

Criticism—Its Effect Upon Mr. Lincoln—A Bull-frog Story He Told as an Illustration.

Violent criticism, attacks and denunciations, coming either from radicals or conservatives, rarely ruffled the President, if they reached his ears. It must have been in connection with something of this kind, that he once told a friend this story:

"Some years ago, ' said he, "a couple of 'emigrants,' fresh from the 'Emerald Isle,' seeking labor, were making their way toward the West. Coming suddenly one evening upon a pond of water, they were greeted with a grand chorus of bull-frogs—a kind of music they had never before heard. 'B-a-u-m!'—B-a-u-m!'

"Overcome with terror, they clutched their 'shillelahs,' and crept cautiously forward, straining their eyes in every direction to catch a glimpse of the enemy; but he was not to be found!

"At last a happy idea seized the foremost one—he sprang to his companion and exclaimed, 'And sure, Jamie! it is my opinion it's *nothing but a 'noise!'* "

Lincoln's Story of a Poodle Dog Used on the End of a Long Pole to Swab Windows.

A friend who was walking over from the White House to the War Department with Mr. Lincoln, repeated to him the story of a "contraband" who had fallen into the hands of some good, pious people, and was being taught by them to read and pray.

Going off by himself one day, he was overheard to commence a prayer by the introduction of himself as "Jim Williams—a berry good nigga' to wash windows; 'spec's you know me now?"

After a hearty laugh at what he called this "direct way of putting the case," Mr. Lincoln said:

"The story that suggests to me, has no resemblance to it, save in the 'washing windows' part. A lady in Philadelphia had a pet poodle dog, which mysteriously disappeared. Rewards were offered for him, and a great ado made without effect. Some weeks passed, and all hope of the favorite's return had been given up, when a servant brought him in one day in the filthiest condition imaginable. The lady was overjoyed to see her pet again, but horrified at his appearance.

' Where *did* you find him ? ' she exclaimed.

" ' Oh,' replied the man, very unconcernedly, ' a negro down the street had him tied to the end of a pole, *swabbing* windows.' "

Lincoln's Little Speech to the Union League Committee — No Swapping Horses in the River.

The day following the adjournment at Baltimore, various political organizations called to pay their respects to the President. First came the convention committee, embracing one from each state represented—appointed to announce to him, formally, the nomination. Next came the Ohio delegation, with Menter's Band, of Cincinnati. Following these were the representatives of the National Union League, to whom he said, in concluding his brief response :

" I do not allow myself to suppose that either the convention or the League have concluded to decide that I am either the greatest or the best man in America; but, rather, they have concluded that it is not best to *swap* horses while crossing the river, and have further concluded that I am not so poor a horse, but that they might make a *botch* of it in trying to *swap!* "

Ejecting a Cashiered Officer from the White House — Mr. Lincoln Much Offended and How He Acted.

Among the callers at the White House one day, was an officer who had been cashiered from the service. He had prepared an elaborate defence of himself, which he consumed much time in reading to the President. When he had finished, Mr. Lincoln replied, that even upon his own statement of the case, the facts would not warrant executive interference. Disappointed and considerably crestfallen, the man withdrew.

8

A few days afterward he made a second attempt to alter the President's convictions, going over substantially the same ground, and occupying about the same space of time, but without accomplishing his end.

The *third* time he succeeded in forcing himself into Mr. Lincoln's presence, who with great forbearance listened to another repetition of the case to its conclusion, but made no reply. Waiting for a moment, the man gathered from the expression of his countenance that his mind was unconvinced. Turning very abruptly, he said :

" Well, Mr. President, I see you are fully determined not to do me justice ! "

This was too aggravating, even for Mr. Lincoln. Manifesting, however, no more feeling than that indicated by a slight compression of the lips, he very quietly arose, laid down a package of papers he held in his hand, and then suddenly seizing the defunct officer by the coat-collar, he marched him forcibly to the door, saying, as he ejected him into the passage :

"Sir, I give you fair warning never to show yourself in this room again. I can bear censure, but not insult ! "

In a whining tone the man begged for his papers, which he had dropped.

" Begone, sir," said the President, " your papers will be sent to you. I never wish to see your face again ! "

Lincoln and the Wall Street Gold Gamblers — He Wishes their "Devilish Heads Shot Off."

Mr. Carpenter, the artist, is responsible for the following:

The bill empowering the Secretary of the Treasury to sell the surplus gold had recently passed, and Mr. Chase was then in New York, giving his attention personally to the experiment. Governor Curtin referred to this, saying to the President :

"I see by the quotations that Chase's movement has already knocked gold down several per cent."

This gave occasion for the strongest expression I ever heard fall from the lips of Mr. Lincoln. Knotting his face in the intensity of his feeling, he said : "Curtin, what do you think of those fellows in Wall Street, who are gambling in gold at such a time as this ?"

"They are a set of sharks," returned Curtin.

"For my part," continued the President, bringing his clinched hand down upon the table, "I wish every one of them had his *devilish head shot off!*"

How the Negroes Regarded " Massa Linkum " — A Story that Deeply Impressed the President.

In 1863, Colonel McKaye, of New York, with Robert Dale Owen and one or two other gentlemen, were associated as a committee to investigate the condition of the freedmen on the coast of North Carolina. Upon their return from Hilton Head they reported to the President; and in the course of the interview Colonel McKaye related the following incident:

He had been speaking of the ideas of power entertained by these people. He said they had an idea of God, as the Almighty, and they had realized in their former condition the power of their masters. Up to the time of the arrival among them of the Union forces, they had no knowledge of any other power. Their masters fled upon the approach of our soldiers, and this gave the slaves a. conception of a power greater than that exercised by them. This power they called " Massa Linkum."

Colonel McKaye said that their place of worship was a large building which they called " the praise house : " and the leader of the meeting, a venerable black man, was known as " the praise man." On a certain day, when there was quite a large gathering of the people, considerable confusion was created by different persons attempting to tell who and what " Massa Linkum " was. In the midst of the excitement the white-headed leader commanded silence.

" Brederin," said he, " you don't know nosen' what you'se talkin' 'bout. Now, you just listen to me. Massa Linkum, he eberywhar. He know eberyting." Then, solemnly looking up, he added,—" *He walk de earf like de Lord !* "

Colonel McKaye said that Mr. Lincoln seemed much affected by this account. He did not smile, as another man might have done, but got up from his chair and walked in silence two or three times across the floor. As he resumed his seat, he said very impressively:

" It is a momentous thing to be the instrument, under Providence, of the liberation of a race."

One of Lincoln's Last Stories.

One of the last stories heard from Mr. Lincoln was concerning John Tyler, for whom it was to be expected, as an old Henry Clay Whig, he would entertain no great respect. " A year or two after Tyler's accession to the Presidency," said he, " contemplating an excursion in some direction, his son went to order a special train of cars. It so happened that the railroad superintendent was a very strong Whig. On 'Bob's ' making known his errand, that official bluntly informed him that his road did not run any special trains for the President.

" ' What!' said ' Bob,' ' did you not furnish a special train for the funeral of General Harrison?'

" ' Yes,' said the superintendent, stroking his whiskers; ' and if you will only bring your father here in *that* shape, you shall have the best train on the road!' "

Lincoln's Habits in the White House—The Same " Old Abe "—A Laughable Glove Story.

Mr. Lincoln's habits at the White House were as simple as they were at his old home in Illinois. He never alluded to himself as " President," or as occupying " the Presidency." His office, he always designated as " this place." " Call me Lincoln," said he to a friend—" Mr. President " had become so very tiresome to him. " If you see a newsboy down the street, send him up this way," said he to a passenger, as he stood waiting for the morning news at his gate. Friends cautioned him against exposing himself so openly in the midst of enemies; but he never heeded them. He frequently walked the streets at night, entirely unprotected; and he felt any check upon his free movements as a great annoyance. He delighted to see his familiar Western friends; and he gave them always a cordial welcome. He met them on the old footing, and fell at once into the accustomed habits of talk and story-telling.

An old acquaintance, with his wife, visited Washington. Mr. and Mrs. Lincoln proposed to these friends a ride in the Presidential carriage. It should be stated, in advance, that the two men had probably never seen each other with gloves on in their lives, unless when they were used as protection from the cold.

The question of each—Mr. Lincoln at the White House, and his friend at the hotel—was, whether he should wear gloves. Of course, the ladies urged gloves; but Mr. Lincoln only put his in his pocket, to be used or not, according to circumstances.

When the Presidential party arrived at the hotel, to take in their friends, they found the gentleman, overcome by his wife's persuasions, very handsomely gloved. The moment he took his seat, he began to draw off the clinging kids, while Mr. Lincoln began to draw his on!

"No! no! no!" protested his friend, tugging at his gloves. "It is none of my doings; put up your gloves, Mr. Lincoln."

So the two old friends were on even and easy terms, and had their ride after their old fashion.

Lincoln's High Compliment to the Women of America.

A Fair for the benefit of the soldiers, held at the Patent Office, in Washington, called out Mr. Lincoln as an interested visitor; and he was not permitted to retire without giving a word to those in attendance. "In this extraordinary war," said he, "extraordinary developments have manifested themselves, such as have not been seen in former wars; and among these manifestations nothing has been more remarkable than these fairs for the relief of suffering soldiers and their families. And the chief agents in these fairs are the women of America. I am not accustomed to the use of language of eulogy; I have never studied the art of paying compliments to women; but I must say that if all that has been said by orators and poets, since the creation of the world, in praise of women, were applied to the women of America, it would not do them justice for their conduct during the war. I will close by saying, God bless the women of America!"

Lincoln in the Hour of Deep Sorrow—He Recalls His Mother's Prayers.

In February, 1862, Mr. Lincoln was visited by a severe affliction in the death of his beautiful son, Willie, and the extreme illness of his son, Thomas, familiarly called "Tad." This was a new burden, and the visitation which, in his firm faith in Providence, he regarded as providential, was also inexplicable. A Christian lady from Massachusetts, who was officiating as nurse in one of the hospitals at the time, came to attend the sick children. She reports that Mr. Lincoln watched with her about the bedside of the sick ones, and that he often walked the room, saying, sadly:

"This is the hardest trial of my life; why is it? Why is it?"

In the course of conversations with her, he questioned her concerning his situation. She told Him that she was a widow, and that her husband and two children were in heaven; and added that she saw the hand of God in it all, and that she had never loved Him so much before as she had since her affliction.

"How is that brought about?" inquired Mr. Lincoln.

"Simply by trusting in God, and feeling that He does all things well," she replied.

"Did you submit fully under the first loss?" he asked.

"No," she answered, "not wholly; but, as blow came upon blow, and all were taken, I could and did submit, and was very happy."

He responded: "I am glad to hear you say that. Your experience will help me to bear my affliction."

On being assured that many Christians were praying for him on the morning of the funeral, he wiped away the tears that sprang in his eyes, and said:

"I am glad to hear that. I want them to pray for me. I need their prayers."

As he was going out to the burial, the good lady expressed her sympathy with him. He thanked her gently, and said:

"I will try to go to God with my sorrows."

A few days afterward, she asked him if he could trust God. He replied:

"I think I can, and I will try. I wish I had that child-like faith you speak of, and I trust He will give it to me."

And then he spoke of his mother, whom so many years before he had committed to the dust among the wilds of Indiana. In this hour of his great trial, the memory of her who had held him upon her bosom, and soothed his childish griefs, came back to him with tenderest recollections. " I remember her prayers," said he, " *and they have always followed me. They have clung to me all my life.*"

A Praying President — "Prayer and Praise."

After the second defeat at Bull Run, Mr. Lincoln appeared very much distressed about the number of killed and wounded, and said to a lady friend : " I have done the best I could. I have asked God to guide me, and now I must leave the event with him."

On another occasion, having been made acquainted with the fact that a great battle was in progress, at a distant but important point, he came into the room where this lady was engaged in nursing a member of the family, looking worn and haggard, and saying that he was so anxious that he could eat nothing. The possibility of defeat depressed him greatly ; but the lady told him he must trust, and that he could at least pray.

"Yes," said he, and taking up a Bible, he started for his room.

Could all the people of the nation have overheard the earnest petition that went up from that inner chamber, as it reached the ears of the nurse, they would have fallen upon their knees with tearful and reverential sympathy.

At one o'clock in the afternoon, a telegram reached him announcing a Union victory ; and then he came directly to the room, his face beaming with joy, saying :

"Good news! Good news! The victory is ours, and God is good."

"Nothing like prayer," suggested the pious lady, who traced a direct connection between the event and the prayer which preceded it.

"Yes, there is," he replied—"praise—prayer and praise."

The good lady who communicates these incidents, closes them with the words : " I do believe he was a true Christian, though he had very little confidence in himself."

Telling a Story and Pardoning a Soldier—How Lincoln did Both.

General Fisk attending the reception at the White House, on one occasion saw, waiting in the ante-room, a poor old man from Tennessee. Sitting down beside him, he inquired his errand, and learned that he had been waiting three or four days to get an audience, and that on his seeing Mr. Lincoln probably depended the life of his son, who was under sentence of death for some military offense.

General Fisk wrote his case in outline on a card, and sent it in, with a special request that the President would see the man. In a moment the order came ; and past senators, governors and generals, waiting impatiently, the old man went into the President's presence.

He showed Mr. Lincoln his papers, and he, on taking them, said he would look into the case and give him the result on the following day.

The old man, in an agony of apprehension, looked up into the President's sympathetic face, and actually cried out:

"To-morrow may be too late ! My son is under sentence of death ! The decision ought to be made now !" and the streaming tears told how much he was moved.

"Come," said Mr. Lincoln, "wait a bit, and I'll tell you

a story;" and then he told the old man General Fisk's story about the swearing driver, as follows:

The General had begun his military life as a Colonel, and, when he raised his regiment in Missouri, he proposed to his men that he should do all the swearing of the regiment. They assented ; and for months no instance was known of the violation of the promise. The Colonel had a teamster named John Todd, who, as roads were not always the best, had some difficulty in commanding his temper and his tongue. John happened to be driving a mule-team through a series of mud-holes a little worse than usual, when, unable to restrain himself any longer, he burst forth into a volley of energetic oaths. The Colonel took notice of the offense, and brought John to an account.

"John," said he, "didn't you promise to let me do all the swearing of the regiment ? "

"Yes, I did, Colonel," he replied, "but the fact was the swearing had to be done *then* or not at all, and *you weren't there to do it.*"

As he told the story, the old man forgot his boy, and both the President and his listener had a hearty laugh together at its conclusion. Then he wrote a few words which the old man read, and in which he found new occasion for tears; but the tears were tears of joy, for the words saved the life of his son.

In all the great emergencies of his closing years, Mr. Lincoln's reliance upon Divine guidance and assistance was often extremely touching.

" I have been driven many times to my knees," he once remarked, " by the overwhelming conviction that I had nowhere else to go. My own wisdom, and that of all about me, seemed insufficient for that day."

THE NATIONAL LINCOLN MONUMENT.

In Oak Ridge Cemetery, at Springfield, Ill. The base of this monument is 72½ ft. square, and with the circular projection of the catacomb on the north, and memorial hall on the south, the extreme length on the ground from north to south is 119½ ft. Height of terrace, 15 ft. and 10 in. From the terrace to the apex of the obelisk, 82 ft. 6½ in. From the grade line to the top of the four round pedestals, 28 ft. 4 in., and to the top of the pedastal of the Lincoln Statue, 35½ ft. Total height from ground line to apex of obelisk, 98 ft. 4½ in. Total expense of erection, about $200,000.

WAR STORIES.

**Lincoln's War Story of Andy Johnson.—Andy Seeks a Doubtful
Interest in Col. Moody's Prayers.**

Col. Moody, " the fighting Methodist parson," as he was
called in Tennessee, while attending a conference in Philadelphia, met the President and related to him the following
story, which we give as repeated by Mr. Lincoln to a friend:

" He told me," said Lincoln, " this story of Andy Johnson and General Buel, which interested me intensely. The
Colonel happened to be in Nashville the day it was reported
that Buel had decided to evacuate the city. The Rebels,
strongly re-enforced, were said to be within two days' march
of the capital. Of course, the city was greatly excited.
Moody said he went in search of Johnson, at the edge of
the evening, and found him at his office, closeted with two
gentlemen, who were walking the floor with him, one on
each side. As he entered they retired, leaving him alone
with Johnson, who came up to him, manifesting intense
feeling, and said, ' Moody, we are sold out! Buel is a
traitor! He is going to evacuate the city, and in forty-
eight hours we will all be in the hands of the Rebels!'
Then he commenced pacing the floor again, twisting his
hands, and chafing like a caged tiger, utterly insensible to
his friend's entreaties to become calm. Suddenly he turned
and said:

" ' Moody, can you pray?'

" ' That is my business, sir, as a minister of the Gospel,'
returned the Colonel.

" ' Well, Moody, I wish you would pray,' said Johnson;

and instantly both went down upon their knees, at opposite sides of the room.

As the prayer waxed fervent, Johnson began to respond in true Methodist style. Presently he crawled over on his hands and knees to Moody's side, and put his arm over him, manifesting the deepest emotion. Closing the prayer with a hearty ' Amen' from each, they arose.

"Johnson took a long breath, and said, with emphasis, ' Moody, I feel better!' Shortly afterwards he asked, ' Will you stand by me ?'

"'Certainly, I will,' was the answer.

"'Well, Moody, I can depend upon you; you are one in a hundred thousand!' He then commenced pacing the floor again. Suddenly he wheeled, the current of his thought having changed, and said, 'Oh! Moody, I don't want you to think I have become a religious man because I asked you to pray. I am sorry to say it, but I am not, and have never pretended to be, religious. No one knows this better than you ; but, Moody, there is one thing about it—I DO believe in ALMIGHTY GOD ! And I believe also in the BIBLE, and I say d——n me, if Nashville shall be surrendered !'"

And Nashville was not surrendered.

A Soldier that Knew no Royalty.

Captain Mix, the commander, at one period, of the President's body-guard, told this story to a friend:

On their way to town one sultry morning, from the Soldier's Home, they came upon a regiment marching into the city. A "straggler," very heavily loaded with camp equipage, was accosted by the President with the question:

"My lad, what is that?" referring to the designation of his regiment.

" It's a regiment," said the soldier, curtly, plodding on, his gaze bent steadily upon the ground.

" Yes, I see that," rejoined the President, " but I want to know *what* regiment."

" —— Pennsylvania," replied the man in the same tone, looking neither to the right nor the left.

As the carriage passed on, Mr. Lincoln turned to Captain Mix and said, with a merry laugh, " It is very evident that chap smells no blood of ' *royalty* ' in this establishment."

A Little Soldier Boy that Lincoln Wanted to Bow to.

" President Lincoln," says the Hon. W. D. Kell, " was a large and many-sided man, and yet so simple that no one, not even a child, could approach him without feeling that he had found in him a sympathizing friend. I remember that I apprised him of the fact that a lad, the son of one of my townsmen, had served a year on board the gunboat *Ottawa*, and had been in two important engagements; in the first as a powder-monkey, when he had conducted himself with such coolness that he had been chosen as captain's messenger in the second; and I suggested to the President that it was in his power to send to the Naval School, annually, three boys who had served at least a year in the navy.

" He at once wrote on the back of a letter from the commander of the *Ottawa*, which I had handed him, to the Secretary of the Navy: ' If the appointments for this year have not been made, let this boy be appointed.' The appointment had not been made, and I brought it home with me. It directed the lad to report for examination at the school in July. Just as he was ready to start, his father, looking over the law, discovered that he could not report until he was fourteen years of age, which he would not be until September following. The poor child sat down and wept. He feared that he was not to go to the Naval School. He was, however, soon consoled by being told that ' the President could make it right.' It was my fortune to meet him the next morning at the door of the Executive Chamber with his father.

"Taking by the hand the little fellow—short for his age, dressed in the sailor's blue pants and shirt—I advanced with him to the President, who sat in his usual seat, and said:

" ' Mr. President, my young friend, Willie Bladen, finds a difficulty about his appointment. You have directed him to appear at the school in July; but he is not yet fourteen years of age.' But before I got half of this out, Mr. Lincoln, laying down his spectacles, rose and said:

" ' Bless me! is that the boy who did so gallantly in those two great battles? Why, I feel that I should bow to him, and not he to me.' The little fellow had made his graceful bow.

"The President took the papers at once, and as soon as he learned that a postponement until September would suffice, made the order that the lad should report in that month. Then putting his hand on Willie's head, he said:

" ' Now, my boy, go home and have good fun during the two months, for they are about the last holiday you will get.' The little fellow bowed himself out, feeling that the President of the United States, though a very great man, was one that he would nevertheless like to have a game of romps with."

The Story of Sallie Ward's Practical Philosophy.

When the telegram from Cumberland Gap reached Mr. Lincoln that " firing was heard in the direction of Knoxville," he remarked that he " was glad of it." Some person present, who had the perils of Burnside's position uppermost in his mind, could not see *why* Mr. Lincoln should be *glad* of it, and so expressed himself.

"Why, you see," responded the President, "it reminds me of Mrs. Sallie Ward, a neighbor of mine, who had a very large family. Occasionally one of her numerous progeny would be heard crying in some out-of-the-way place, upon which Mrs. Ward would exclaim:

'*There's one of my children that isn't dead yet.*' "

Lincoln While in Bed Pardons a Soldier.

The Hon. Mr. Kellogg, representative from Essex County, New York, received a dispatch one evening from the army, to the effect that a young townsman, who had been induced to enlist through his instrumentality, had, for a serious misdemeanor, been convicted by a court-martial, and was to be shot the next day. Greatly agitated, Mr. Kellogg went to the Secretary of War, and urged, in the strongest manner, a reprieve. Stanton was inexorable.

"Too many cases of the kind had been let off," he said, "and it was time an example was made."

Exhausting his eloquence in vain, Mr. Kellogg said: "Well, Mr. Secretary, the boy is not going to be *shot*—of that I give you fair warning!"

Leaving the War Department, he went directly to the White House, although the hour was late. The sentinel on duty told him that special orders had been issued to admit no one whatever that night. After a long parley, by pledging himself to assume the responsibility of the act, the congressman passed in. The President had retired, but, indifferent to etiquette or ceremony, Judge Kellogg pressed his way through all obstacles to his sleeping apartment.

In an excited manner he stated that the dispatch announcing the hour of execution had but just reached him.

"This man must not be shot, Mr. President," said he. "I can't help what he may have done. Why, he is an old neighbor of mine; I can't allow him to be shot!"

Mr. Lincoln had remained in bed, quietly listening to the vehement protestations of his old friend (they were in Congress together). He at length said: "Well, I don't believe *shooting* him will do him any good. Give me that pen." And, so saying, "red tape" was unceremoniously cut, and another poor fellow's lease of life was indefinitely extended.

What Lincoln Considered the "Great Event of the Nineteenth Century."—Lincoln's Vow Before God.

The following incident, remarkable for its significant facts, is related by Mr. Carpenter, the artist :

Mr. Chase, says Mr. Carpenter, told me that at the Cabinet meeting immediately after the battle of Antietam, and just prior to the issue of the September proclamation, the President entered upon the business before them, by saying that "the time for the annunciation of the emancipation policy could be no longer delayed. Public sentiment would sustain it—many of his warmest friends and supporters demanded it—*and he had promised his God he would do it !*" The last part of this was uttered in a low tone, and appeared to be heard by no one but Secretary Chase, who was sitting near him. He asked the President if he correctly understood him. Mr. Lincoln replied : "*I made a solemn vow before God that if Gen. Lee was driven back from Pennsylvania, I would crown the result by the declaration of freedom to the slaves.*"

In February, 1865, a few days after the Constitutional Amendment, I went to Washington, and was received by

Mr. Lincoln with the kindness and familiarity which had characterized our previous intercourse. I said to him at this time that I was very proud to have been the artist to have first conceived of the design of painting a picture commemorative of the Act of Emancipation ; that subsequent occurrences had only confirmed my own first judgment of that act as the most sublime moral event in our history. "Yes," said he,—and never do I remember to have noticed in him more earnestness of expression or manner,—" as affairs have turned, *it is the central act of my administration, and the great event of the nineteenth century.*"

Lincoln Proposes to "Borrow the Army" from one of his Generals.

On a certain occasion the President said to a friend that he was in great distress; he had been to General McClellan's house, and the General did not ask to see him; and as he must talk to somebody, he had sent for General Franklin and myself, to obtain our opinion as to the possibility of soon commencing active operations with the Army of the Potomac. To use his own expression, if something was not soon done, the bottom would fall out of the whole affair; and if General McClellan did not want to use the army, he would like to *borrow it*, provided he could see how it could be made to do something.

Lincoln Could not Allow a Soldier to be More Polite than Himself.

I was always touched, says Mr. Carpenter, by the President's manner of receiving the salute of the guard at the White House. Whenever he appeared in the portico, on his way to or from the War or Treasury Department, or on any excursion down the avenue, the first glimpse of him

was, of course, the signal for the sentinel on duty to
" present arms," and " call out the guard."

This was always acknowledged by Mr. Lincoln with a
peculiar bow and touch of the hat, no matter how many
times it might occur in the course of a day ; and it always
seemed to me as much a compliment to the devotion of the
soldiers, on his part, as it was the sign of duty and deference
on the part of the guard.

An Interesting Visit to the Hospitals—How the Soldiers Received Him—He Meets a Wounded Confederate who Asks His Pardon—The President Weeps.

" On the Monday before the assassination, when the President was on his return from Richmond, he stopped at City
Point. Calling upon the head surgeon at that place, Mr.
Lincoln told him that he wished to visit all the hospitals
under his charge, and shake hands with every soldier. The
surgeon asked if he knew what he was undertaking, there
being five or six thousand soldiers at that place, and it
would be quite a tax upon his strength to visit all the wards
and shake hands with every soldier. Mr. Lincoln answered,
with a smile, he ' guessed he was equal to the task; at any
rate he would try, and go as far as he could; he should
never, probably, see the boys again, and he wanted them to
know that he appreciated what they had done for their
country.'

" Finding it useless to try to dissuade him, the surgeon
began his rounds with the President, who walked from bed
to bed, extending his hand to all, saying a few words of
sympathy to some, making kind inquiries of others, and
welcomed by all with the heartiest cordiality.

"As they passed along, they came to a ward in which
lay a rebel who had been wounded and was a prisoner. As

the tall figure of the kindly visitor appeared in sight, he was recognized by the rebel soldier, who, raising himself on his elbow in bed, watched Mr. Lincoln as he approached, and extending his hand exclaimed, while tears ran down his cheeks,—

" ' Mr. Lincoln, I have long wanted to see you, to ask your forgiveness for ever raising my hand against the old flag.'

" Mr. Lincoln was moved to tears. He heartily shook the hand of the repentant rebel, and assured him of his good will, and with a few words of kind advice passed on. "After some hours the tour of the various hospitals was made, and Mr. Lincoln returned with the surgeon to his office. They had scarcely entered, however, when a messenger came saying that one ward had been omitted, and ' the boys ' wanted to see the President. The surgeon, who was thoroughly tired, and knew Mr. Lincoln must be, tried to dissuade him from going; but the good man said he must go back; he would not knowingly omit one, ' the boys ' would be so disappointed. So he went with the messenger, accompanied by the surgeon, and shook hands with the gratified soldiers, and then returned again to the office.

" The surgeon expressed the fear that the President's arm would be lamed with so much hand-shaking, saying that it certainly must ache. Mr. Lincoln smiled, and saying something about his ' strong muscles,' stepped out at the open door, took up a very large, heavy axe which lay there by a log of wood, and chopped vigorously for a few moments, sending the chips flying in all directions; and then, pausing, he extended his right arm to its full length, holding the axe out horizontally, without its even quivering as he held it. Strong men who looked on—men accustomed to manual labor—could not hold the same axe in that position for a moment. Returning to the office, he took a glass of lemonade, for he would take no stronger beverage; and while he was within, the chips he had chopped were gathered up and safely cared for by a hospital steward, because they were 'the chips that Father Abraham chopped.' "

Mr. Lincoln and a Clergyman.

At the semi-annual meeting of the New Jersey Historical Society, held recently in Newark, N. J., Rev. Dr. Sheldon, of Princeton, read a memorial of their late President, Rev. R. K. Rodgers, D.D., in which appears the following fresh incident concerning Mr. Lincoln and the war:

"One day during the war, Dr. Rodgers was called on by a man in his congregation, who, in the greatest distress, told him that his son, a soldier in the army, had just been sentenced to be shot for desertion, and begged the minister's interposition. The Doctor went to Washington with the wife and infant child of the condemned man, and sent his card up to Mr. Lincoln. When admitted, the President said:

"'You are a minister, I believe. What can I do for you, my friend?'

"The reply was: 'A young man from my congregation in the army has so far forgotten his duty to his country and his God as to desert his colors, and is sentenced to die. I have come to ask you to spare him.'

'With characteristic quaintness the President replied: 'Then you don't want him hurt, do you?'

"'Oh, no,' said the petitioner, I did not mean that; he deserves punishment, but I beg for him time to prepare to meet his God.'

"'Do you say he has father, wife and child?' said Mr. Lincoln. "'Yes.' "'Where do you say he is?'

" On being told, he turned to his secretary, said a few words in an undertone, of which that official made note, and added to Dr. Rodgers, ' You have your request. Tell his friends I have reprieved him.'

" With a ' God bless you, Mr. President,' Dr. Rodgers turned away to bear the glad news to the distressed family."

A Remarkable Letter From Lincoln to Gen. Hooker.

The following remarkable letter from Lincoln to General Hooker was written after the latter had taken command of the Army of the Potomac, in January, 1863, and while the President yet retained it in his possession, an intimate friend chanced to be in his Cabinet one night, and the President read it to him, remarking, "I shall not read this to anybody else, but I want to know how it strikes you." During the following April or May, while the Army of the Potomac lay opposite Fredericksburg, this friend accompanied the President to General Hooker's headquarters on a visit. One night General Hooker, alone in his tent with this gentleman, said:

" The President says that he showed you this letter," and he then took out that document, which was closely written on a sheet of letter-paper. The tears stood in the General's bright blue eyes as he added: " It is such a letter as a father might have written to his son. And yet it hurt me." Then, dashing the water from his eyes, he said: " When I have been to Richmond, I shall have this letter published."

This was more than sixteen years ago, and the letter has just now seen the light of day. There are in it certain sharp passages which, after this long lapse of time, can not be verified by the memory of any who heard it read in 1863. There are others which seem missing. Nevertheless, the letter, which is herewith reprinted, must have been written by Lincoln:

EXECUTIVE MANSION, WASHINGTON, D. C., Jan. 26, 1863.—*Maj.-Gen. Hooker*—GENERAL: I have placed you at the head of the Army of the Potomac. Of course I have done this upon what appears to me to be sufficient reasons; and yet I think it best for you to know that there are some things in regard to which I am not quite satisfied with you. I believe you to be a brave and skillful soldier—which, of course, I like. I also believe you do not mix politics with your profession—in which you are right. You have confidence in yourself—which is a valuable, if not an indispensable, quality. You are ambitious—which, within reasonable bounds, does good rather than harm; but I think that, during General Burnside's command of the army, you have taken counsel of your ambition and thwarted him as much as you could, in which you did a great wrong to the country, and to a most meritorious and honorable brother-officer. I have heard, in such a way as to believe it, of your recently saying that both the army and the Government needed a Dictator. Of course, it was not for this, but in spite of it, that I have given you the command. Only those Generals who gain successes can set up Dictators. What I now ask of you is military success, and I will risk the Dictatorship. The Government will support you to the utmost of its ability—which is neither more nor less than it has done and will do for all commanders. I much fear that the spirit which you have aided to infuse into the army, of criticising their commander and withholding confidence from him, will now turn upon you. I shall assist you as far as I can to put it down. Neither you nor Napoleon, if he were alive again, could get any good out of an army while such a spirit prevails in it. And now beware of rashness. Beware of rashness, but, with energy and sleepless vigilance, go forward and give us victories. Yours, very truly,   A. LINCOLN.

An Amusing Anecdote of a "Hen-Pecked Husband."

When General Phelps took possession of Ship Island, near New Orleans, early in the war, it will be remembered that he issued a proclamation, somewhat bombastic in tone, freeing the slaves. To the surprise of many people, on both sides, the President took no official notice of this movement. Some time had elapsed, when one day a friend took

DOUGLAS MONUMENT.

On the banks of Lake Michigan, near foot of 35th Street, Chicago, in the midst of a beautiful park. It is built of granite from Hollowell, Me., with an altitude of 104 feet, and at an expense of about $100,000. Douglas and Lincoln began public life together as members of the Illinois Legislature. Though differing in political faith, they were really life-long friends.

him to task for his seeming indifference on so important a matter.

"Well," said Mr. Lincoln, " I feel about that a good deal as a man whom I will call ' Jones,' whom I once knew, did about his wife. He was one of your meek men, and had the reputation of being badly hen-pecked. At last, one day his wife was seen switching him out of the house. A day or two afterward a friend met him in the street, and said: ' Jones, I have always stood up for you, as you know; but I am not going to do it any longer. Any man who will stand quietly and take a switching from his wife, deserves to be horsewhipped.' Jones looked up with a wink, patting his friend on the back. ' Now *don't*,' said he; ' why, it didn't *hurt* me any; and you've no idea what a *power* of *good* it did Sarah Ann ?' "

Lincoln's Curt Reply to a Clergyman.

No nobler reply ever fell from the lips of a ruler, than that uttered by President Lincoln in response to the clergyman who ventured to say, in his presence during the war, that he *hoped* "the Lord was on our side."

"I am not at all concerned about that," replied Mr. Lincoln, " for I know that the Lord is *always* on the side of the *right*. But it is my constant anxiety and prayer that *I* and *this nation* should be on the Lord's *side*."

A Short Practical Sermon.

" On a certain occasion, two ladies, from Tennessee, came before the President, asking the release of their husbands, held as prisoners of war at Johnson's Island. They were put off until the following Friday, when they came again, and were again put off until Saturday. At each of the interviews one of the ladies urged that her husband was a religious man. On Saturday, when the President ordered the release of the prisoner, he said to this lady:

"'You say your husband is a religious man; tell him, when you meet him, that I say I am not much of a judge of religion, but that in my opinion the religion which sets men to rebel and fight against their Government, because, as they think, that Government does not sufficiently help *some* men to eat their bread in the sweat of *other* men's faces, is not the sort of religion upon which people can get to heaven.'"

A Celebrated Case Settled with Lincoln-like Celerity.

The celebrated case of Franklin W. Smith and brother, was one of those which most largely helped to bring military tribunals into public contempt. Those two gentlemen were arrested and kept in confinement, their papers seized, their business destroyed, their reputation damaged, and a naval court-martial, "organized to convict," pursued them unrelentingly till a wiser and juster hand arrested the malice of their persecutors. It is known that President Lincoln, after full investigation of the case, annulled the whole proceedings, but it is remarkable that the actual record of his decision could never be obtained from the Navy Department. An exact copy being withheld, the following was presented to the Boston Board of Trade as being very nearly the words of the late President:

"*Whereas*, Franklin W. Smith had transactions with the Navy Department to the amount of one million and a quarter of a million of dollars; and, *whereas*, he had the chance to steal a quarter of a million, and was only charged with stealing twenty-two hundred dollars—and the question now is about his stealing a hundred—I don't believe he stole anything at all. Therefore, the record and findings are disapproved—declared null and void, and the defendants are fully discharged."

" It would be difficult," says the New York *Tribune*, "to sum up the rights and wrongs of the business more briefly than that, or to find a paragraph more characteristically and unmistakably Mr. Lincoln's.

Recollections of the War President by Judge William Johnston.

I rendered, says Judge Johnston, Mr. Lincoln some service in my time. When I went to Washington I observed that among Congressmen, and others in high places, Mr. Lincoln had very few friends. Montgomery Blair was the only one I heard speak of him for a second term. This was about the middle of his first Administration. I went to Washington by way of Columbus, and G. Tod asked me to carry a verbal message to Mr. Lincoln, and that was to tell him that there were certain elements indispensable to the success of the war that would be seriously affected by any interference with McClellan.

I suppose that the liberal translation of Tod's language would be thus : " I am keeping the Democratic soldiers in the field, and if McClellan is interfered with I shall not be able to do it." We all felt some trouble about it. McClellan had been relieved, and one bright moonlight night I saw a regiment, I suppose Pennsylvanians mostly, marching from the Capitol down Pennsylvania Avenue, yelling at the top of their lungs, " Hurrah for Little Mac ! " and, making a pause before the White House, they kept up that bawling and hurrahing for McClellan.

I went to see Mr. Lincoln early the next morning, and asked him if he had witnessed the performance on the previous night. He said he had. I asked him what he thought of it. He said it was very perplexing. I told him I had come to make a suggestion. I told him I would introduce him to a young man of fine talents and liberal education, who had lost an arm in the service, and I wanted him to tell one of his Cabinet Ministers to give that young man a good place in the Civil Service, and to avail himself of the occasion to declare that the policy of the Administration was, whenever the qualifications were equal, to give those who had been wounded or disabled in the service of the country the preference in the Civil Department. He said it was an idea he would like to think of, and asked me how soon I would wait upon him in the morning. I said any hour; and I went at 7 o'clock and found him in the hands of a barber. Says he: "I have been thinking about your proposition, and I have a question to ask you: Did you ever know Colonel Smith, of Rockford, Ill. ?" I said I had an introduction to him when attending to the defense of Governor Bebb. "You know," said he, "that he was killed at Vicksburg; that his head was carried off by a shell. He was Postmaster, and his wife wants the place," and he inquired if that would come up to my idea; and thereupon he and I concocted a letter—I have the correspondence in my possession—to Postmaster General Blair, directing him to appoint the widow of Colonel Smith Postmistress, in the room of her deceased husband, who had fallen in battle, and stating that in consideration of what was due to the men who were fighting our battles, he had made up his mind that the families of those who had fallen, and those disabled in the service, their qualifications being equal, should always have a preference in the Civil Service.

I told him I was not personally acquainted with Blair, and he gave me a note of introduction to him with the letter. I told Blair that I proposed to take a copy of Mr. Lincoln's letter, which he had then made out by the clerk. I took the letter to the *Chronicle* office in Washington, in which paper it was published, and the next morning I jumped into an ambulance and went to the convalescing camp, where there were about 7,000 convalescents, a great many of them Ohio men, and when I made my appearance they called on me for a speech. I got upon a terrace and made them a few remarks, and, coming round to the old saw, " that Republics are always ungrateful," I told them I could not vouch for the Republic, but I thought I could vouch for the chief man at the head of the Administration, and he had already spoken on that subject, and when I read Lincoln's letter the boys flung their hats into the air and made the welkin ring for a long while. I hurried back to the city, and with a pair of shears cut out Lincoln's letter, and then attached some editorial remarks, and that letter went around, and I believe was published in every friendly newspaper in the United States. About that time Congress passed a resolution to the same effect, that those disabled in the military service of the country, wherever qualified, ought to have a preference over others. This may have been a small matter, but it made a marvelous impression on the army.

The Serpent in Bed With Two Children.

A number of Kentuckians insisted that troops should not be sent through that state for the purpose of putting down the war in Tennessee. The President was hesitating what to do, and they were pressing immediate action.

"I am," he said, "a good deal like the farmer who, returning to his home one Winter night, found his two sweet little boys asleep with a hideous serpent crawling over their bodies. He could not strike the serpent without wounding or killing the children, so he calmly waited until it had moved away. Now, I do not want to act in a hurry about this matter; I don't want to hurt anybody in Kentucky; but I will get the serpent out of Tennessee.

"And he did march through Kentucky, to the aid of Andrew Johnson's mountaineers."

A Church Which God Wanted for the Union Soldiers.

"Among the various applicants at the White House one day was a well-dressed lady, who came forward, without apparent embarrassment in her air of manner, and addressed the President. Giving her a very close and scrutinizing look, he said:

"' Well, madam, what can I do for you?'

" She proceeded to tell him that she lived in Alexandria; that the church where she worshiped had been taken for a hospital.

"' What church, madam?' Mr. Lincoln asked, in a quick, nervous manner.

"' The —— Church,' she replied ; ' and as there are only two or three wounded soldiers in it, I came to see if you would not let us have it, as we want it very much to worship God in.'

"' Madam, have you been to see the Post Surgeon at Alexandria about this matter?'

"' Yes, sir; but we could do nothing with him.'

"' Well, we put him there to attend to just such business, and it is reasonable to suppose that he knows better what should be done under the circumstances than I do. See here: you say you live in Alexandria; probably you own property there. How much will you give to assist in building a hospital?'

"' You know, Mr. Lincoln, our property is very much embarrassed by the war;—so, really, I could hardly afford to give much for such a purpose.'

" ' Well, madam, I expect we shall have another fight soon; and my candid opinion is, *God wants that church for poor wounded Union soldiers,* as much as He does for secesh people to worship in.' Turning to his table, he said, quite abruptly, ' You will excuse me; I can do nothing for you. Good-day, madam.' "

How Lincoln Relieved Rosecrans.

General James B. Steedman, familiarly known as " Old Chickamauga," relates the following: Some weeks after the disastrous battle of Chickamauga, while yet Chattanooga was in a state of siege, General Steedman was surprised one day to receive a telegram from Abraham Lincoln to come to Washington. Seeking out Thomas, he laid the telegram before him, and was instructed to set out at once. Repairing to the White House, he was warmly received by Mr. Lincoln. Mr. Lincoln's first question was abrupt and to the point :

" General Steedman, what is your opinion of General Rosecrans?"

General Steedman, hesitating a moment, said: " Mr. President, I would rather not express my opinion of my superior officer."

Mr. Lincoln said: " It is the man who does not want to express an opinion whose opinion I want. I am besieged on all sides with advice. Every day I get letters from army officers asking me to allow them to come to Washington to impart some valuable knowledge in their possession."

" Well, Mr. President," said General Steedman, " you are the Commander-in-Chief of the Army, and if you order me to speak I will do so."

Mr. Lincoln said: " Then I will order an opinion."

General Steedman then answered: " Since you com-

10

mand me, Mr. President, I will say General Rosecrans is a splendid man to command a victorious army."

"But what kind of a man is he to command a defeated army?" said Mr. Lincoln.

General Steedman in reply said, cautiously: "I think there are two or three men in that army that would be better."

Then, with his quaint humor, Mr. Lincoln propounded this question: "Who, besides yourself, General Steedman. is there in that army who would make a better commander?"

General Steedman said promptly: "General George H. Thomas."

"I am glad to hear you say so," said Mr. Lincoln, "that is my own opinion exactly. But Mr. Stanton is against him, and it was only yesterday that a powerful New York delegation was here to protest against his appointment because he is from a Rebel State and can not be trusted."

Said General Steedman: "A man who will leave his own state (Thomas was a Virginian), his friends, all his associations, to follow the flag of his country, can be trusted in any position to which he may be called." That night the order went forth from Washington relieving General Rosecrans of the command of the Army of the Cumberland and appointing Thomas in his place.

An Interesting Incident Connected With Signing the Emancipation Proclamation.

"The roll containing the Emancipation Proclamation was taken to Mr. Lincoln at noon on the first day of January, 1863, by Secretary Seward and his son Frederick. As it lay unrolled before him, Mr. Lincoln took a pen, dipped it in ink, moved his hand to the place for the signature, held it a moment, and then removed his hand and dropped the pen. After a little hesitation he again took up the pen and went through the same movement as before. Mr. Lincoln then turned to Mr. Seward, and said:

" ' I have been shaking hands since nine o'clock this morning, and my right arm is almost paralyzed. If my name ever goes into history it will be for this act, and my whole soul is in it. If my hand trembles when I sign the Proclamation, all who examine the document hereafter will say, ' He hesitated.'

" He then turned to the table, took up the pen again, and slowly, firmly wrote ' Abraham Lincoln,' with which the whole world is now familiar. He then looked up, smiled, and said: ' *That will do.*' "

A Dream That Was Portentous — What Lincoln said to General Grant About It.

At the Cabinet meeting held the morning of the day of the assassination, it was afterward remembered, a remarkable circumstance occurred. General Grant was present, and during a lull in the discussion the President turned to him and asked if he had heard from General Sherman. General Grant replied that he had not, but was in hourly expectation of receiving despatches from him announcing the surrender of Johnson.

" Well," said the President, " you will hear very soon now, and the news will be important."

" Why do you think so ?" said the General.

" Because," said Mr. Lincoln, " I had a dream last night; and ever since the war began, I have invariably had the same dream before any important military event occurred." He then instanced Bull Run, Antietam, Gettysburg, etc., and said that before each of these events, he had had the same dream; and turning to Secretary Welles, said: "It is in your line, too, Mr. Welles. The dream is, that I saw a ship sailing very rapidly; and I am sure that it portends some important national event."

Later in the day, dismissing all business, the carriage was ordered for a drive. When asked by Mrs. Lincoln if he would like any one to accompany them, he replied:

"No; I prefer to ride by ourselves to-day."

Mrs. Lincoln subsequently said that she never saw him seem so supremely happy as on this occasion. In reply to a remark to this effect, the President said:

"And well I may feel so, Mary, for I consider this day the war has come to a close." And then added: "We must both be more cheerful in the future; between the war and the loss of our darling Willie, we have been very miserable."

Lincoln and Judge Baldwin.

"Judge Baldwin, of California, being in Washington, called one day on General Halleck, and, presuming upon a familiar acquaintance in California a few years before, solicited a pass outside of our lines to see a brother in Virginia, not thinking that he would meet with a refusal, as both his brother and himself were good Union men.

"'We have been deceived too often,' said General Halleck, 'and I regret I can't grant it.'

Judge B. then went to Stanton, and was very briefly disposed of, with the same result. Finally, he obtained an interview with Mr Lincoln, and stated his case.

"'Have you applied to General Halleck?' inquired the President.

"'Yes, and met with a flat refusal,' said Judge B.

" 'Then you must see Stanton,' continued the President.

" ' I have, and with the same result,' was the reply.

" ' Well, then,' said Mr. Lincoln, with a smile, ' I can do nothing; for you must know *that I have very little influence with this Administration.*' "

Lincoln and Stanton Fixing up Peace Between the Two Contending Armies.

" On the night of the 3d of March, the Secretary of War, with others of the Cabinet, were in the company of the President, at the Capitol, awaiting the passage of the final bills of Congress. In the intervals of reading and signing these documents, the military situation was considered—the lively conversation tinged by the confident and glowing account of General Grant, of his mastery of the position, and of his belief that a few days more would see Richmond in our possession, and the army of Lee either dispersed utterly or captured bodily—when the telegram from Grant was received, saying that Lee had asked an interview with reference to peace. Mr. Lincoln was elated, and the kindness of his heart was manifest in intimations of favorable terms to be granted to the conquered Rebels.

" Stanton listened in silence, restraining his emotion, but at length the tide burst forth. ' Mr. President,' said he, ' to-morrow is inauguration day. If you are not to be the President of an obedient and united people, you had better not be inaugurated. Your work is already done, if any other authority than yours is for one moment to be recognized, or any terms made that do not signify you are the supreme head of the nation. If generals in the field are to negotiate peace, or any other chief magistrate is to be acknowledged on this continent, then you are not needed, and you had better not take the oath of office.'

"'Stanton you are right!' said the President, his whole tone changing. 'Let me have a pen.'

"Mr. Lincoln sat down at the table, and wrote as follows :

"'The President directs me to say to you that he wishes you to have no conference with General Lee, unless it be for the capitulation of Lee's army, or on some minor or purely military matter. He instructs me to say that you are not to decide, discuss, or confer upon any political question. Such questions the President holds in his own hands, and will submit them to no military conferences or conventions. In the mean time you are to press to the utmost your military advantages.'

"The President read over what he had written, and then said :

"'Now, Stanton, date and sign this paper, and send it to Grant. We'll see about this peace business.'

"The duty was discharged only too gladly by the energetic Secretary."

The Merciful President.

A personal friend of President Lincoln says : "I called on him one day in the early part of the war. He had just written a pardon for a young man who had been sentenced to be shot, for sleeping at his post, as a sentinel. He remarked as he read it to me :

"'I could not think of going into eternity with the blood of the poor young man on my skirts.' Then he added : 'It is not to be wondered at that a boy, raised on a farm, probably in the habit of going to bed at dark, should, when required to watch, fall asleep; and I can not consent to shoot him for such an act.' "

This story, with its moral, is made complete by Rev. Newman Hall, of London, who, in a sermon preached after and upon Mr. Lincoln's death, says that the dead body of this youth was found among the slain on the field of Fred-

ericksburg, wearing next his heart a photograph of his pre-
server, beneath which the grateful fellow had written, "God
bless President Lincoln!"

From the same sermon another anecdote is gleaned, of a
similar character, which is evidently authentic. An officer
of the army, in conversation with the preacher, said :

" The first week of my command, there were twenty-four
deserters sentenced by court martial to be shot, and the
warrants for their execution were sent to the President to
be signed. He refused. I went to Washington and had an
interview. I said :

" ' Mr. President, unless these men are made an example
of, the army itself is in danger. Mercy to the few is cruelty
to the many.'

" He replied : ' Mr. General, there are already too many
weeping widows in the United States. For God's sake,
don't ask me to add to the number, for I won't do it.' "

No Mercy for the Man Stealer — Lincoln Uses Very Strong Language.

Hon. John B. Alley, of Lynn, Massachusetts, was made
the bearer to the President of a petition for pardon, by a
person confined in the Newburyport jail for being engaged
in the slave-trade. He had been sentenced to five years'
imprisonment, and the payment of a fine of one thousand
dollars. The petition was accompanied by a letter to Mr.
Alley, in which the prisoner acknowledged his guilt and the
justice of his sentence He was very penitent—at least, on
paper — and had received the full measure of his punishment, so far as it related to the term of his imprisonment ;
but he was still held because he could not pay his fine. Mr.
Alley read the letter to the President, who was much moved
by its pathetic appeals ; and when he had himself read the

petition, he looked up and said : " My friend that is a very touching appeal to our feelings. You know my weakness is to be, if possible, too easily moved by appeals for mercy, and, if this man were guilty of the foulest murder that the arm of man could perpetrate, I might forgive him on such an appeal ; but the man who could go to Africa, and rob her of her children, and sell them into interminable bondage, with no other motive than that which is furnished by dollars and cents, is so much worse than the most depraved murderer, that he can never receive pardon at my hands. No ! He may rot in jail before he shall have liberty by any act of mine." A sudden crime, committed under strong temptation, was venial in his eyes, on evidence of repentance ; but the calculating, mercenary crime of man-stealing and man-selling, with all the cruelties that are essential accompaniments of the business, could win from him, as an officer of the people, no pardon.

A Touching Incident in the Life of Lincoln.

A few days before the President's death, Secretary Stanton tendered his resignation of the War Department. He accompanied the act with a heartfelt tribute to Mr. Lincoln's constant friendship and faithful devotion to the country; saying, also, that he as Secretary had accepted the position to hold it only until the war should end, and that now he felt his work was done, and his duty was to resign.

Mr. Lincoln was greatly moved by the Secretary's words, and tearing in pieces the paper containing the resignation, and throwing his arms about the Secretary, he said:

"Stanton, you have been a good friend and a faithful public servant, and it is not for you to say when you will no longer be needed here." Several friends of both parties were present on the occasion, and there was not a dry eye that witnessed the scene.

The Great Thing About Gen. Grant as Lincoln Saw It.

Mr. Carpenter, the artist, made particular inquiry of the President, during the progress of the Battles of the Wilderness, how General Grant personally inpressed him as compared to other officers of the army, and especially those who had been in command.

"The great thing about Grant," said he, " I take it, is his *perfect coolness and persistency of purpose.* I judge he is not easily excited, which is a great element in an officer, and has the *grit* of a bull-dog ! Once let him get his ' teeth ' in, and nothing can shake him off."

Lincoln's Second Nomination—How He Associated it with a Very Singular Circumstance—Lincoln Sees Two Images of Himself in a Mirror.

It appeared that the dispatch announcing Lincoln's renomination for President had been sent to his office from the War Department while he was at lunch. Afterward, without going back to the official chamber, he proceeded to the War Department. While there, the telegram came in announcing the nomination of Johnson.

"What !" said he to the operator, "do they nominate a Vice-President before they do a President?"

" Why!" rejoined the astonished official, " have you not heard of your own nomination? It was sent to the White House two hours ago."

" It is all right," was the reply; " I shall probably find it on my return."

Laughing pleasantly over this incident, he said, soon afterwards : "A very singular occurence took place the day I was nominated at Chicago, four years ago, of which I am reminded to-night. In the afternoon of the day, returning home from down town, I went up-stairs to Mrs.

Lincoln's reading-room. Feeling somewhat tired, I lay down upon a couch in the room, directly opposite a bureau upon which was a looking-glass. As I reclined, my eye fell upon the glass, and *I saw distinctly two images of myself, exactly alike, except that one was a little paler than the other.* I arose, and lay down again, with the same result. It made me quite uncomfortable for a few moments, but some friends coming in, the matter passed out of my mind.

"The next day, while walking in the street, I was suddenly reminded of the circumstance, and the disagreeable sensation produced by it returned. I had never seen anything of the kind before, and did not know what to make of it.

"I determined to go home and place myself in the same position, and if the same effect was produced, I would make up my mind that it was the natural result of some principle of refraction or optics which I did not understand, and dismiss it. I tried the experiment, with a like result; and, as I had said to myself, accounting for it on some principle unknown to me, it ceased to trouble me. But," said he, "some time ago, I tried to produce the same effect *here*, by arranging a glass and couch in the same position, *without success.*"

He did not say, at this time, that either he or Mrs. Lincoln attached any omen to the phenomenon, but it is well known that Mrs. Lincoln regarded it as a sign that the President would be re-elected.

How Lincoln Illustrated What Might Be Done With Jeff. Davis.

One of the latest of Mr. Lincoln's stories, was told to a party of gentlemen, who, among the tumbling ruins of the Confederacy, anxiously asked "what he would do with Jeff. Davis?"

"There was a boy in Springfield," replied Mr. Lincoln, "who saved up his money and bought a 'coon,' which, after the novelty wore off, became a great nuisance.

"He was one day leading him through the streets, and had his hands full to keep clear of the little vixen, who had torn his clothes half off of him. At length he sat down on the curb-stone, completely fagged out. A man passing was stopped by the lad's disconsolate appearance, and asked the matter.

"'Oh,' was the only reply, 'this coon is such a *trouble* to me.'

"'Why don't you get rid of him, then?' said the gentleman.

"'*Hush!*' said the boy; 'don't you see he is gnawing his rope off? I am going to let him do it, and then I will go home and tell the folks *that he got away from me!*'"

Lincoln's Cutting Reply to the Confederate Commission—His Story of "Root Hog or Die."

At a so-called "peace conference" procured by the voluntary and irresponsible agency of Mr. Francis P. Blair, which was held on the steamer River Queen, in Hampton Roads, on the 3d of February, 1865, between President Lincoln and Mr. Seward, representing the government, and Messrs. Alexander H. Stephens, J. A. Campbell and R. M. T. Hunter, representing the rebel confederacy, Mr. Hunter replied that the recognition of Jeff Davis' power was the first and indispensable step to peace; and, to illustrate his point, he referred to the correspondence between King Charles the First and his Parliament, as a reliable precedent of a constitutional ruler treating with rebels. Mr. Lincoln's face wore that indescribable expression which generally preceded his hardest hits; and he remarked:

"Upon questions of history I must refer you to Mr

Seward, for he is posted in such things, and I don't profess to be ; but my only distinct recollection of the matter is that *Charles lost his head !* "

Mr. Hunter remarked, on the same occasion, that the slaves, always accustomed to work upon compulsion, under an overseer, would, if suddenly freed, precipitate not only themselves, but the entire society of the South, into irremediable ruin. No work would be done, but blacks and whites would starve together. The President waited for Mr. Seward to answer the argument, but, as that gentleman hesitated, he said :

" Mr. Hunter, you ought to know a great deal better about this matter than I, for you have always lived under the slave system. I can only say, in reply to your statement of the case, that it reminds me of a man out in Illinois, by the name of Case, who undertook, a few years ago, to raise a very large herd of hogs. It was a great trouble to feed them ; and how to get around this was a puzzle to him. At length he hit upon the plan of planting an immense field of potatoes, and, when they were sufficiently grown, he turned the whole herd into the field and let them have full swing, thus saving not only the labor of feeding the hogs, but that also of digging the potatoes ! Charmed with his sagacity, he stood one day leaning against the fence, counting his hogs, when a neighbor came along :

" ' Well, well,' said he, ' Mr. Case this is all very fine. Your hogs are doing very well just now ; but you know out here in Illinois the frost comes early, and the ground freezes a foot deep. Then what are they going to do ? '

" This was a view of the matter which Mr. Case had not taken into account. Butchering time for hogs was away on in December or January. He scratched his head and at length stammered : ' Well, it may come pretty hard on their *snouts,* but I don't see but it will be *root hog or die!* ' "

HOME OF THE LINCOLNS IN INDIANA.

Located near Gentryville, in Spencer County, and about midway between Evansville and Louisville. The Lincolns emigrated to this point from Kentucky in 1816; they resided here thirteen years.

MISCELLANEOUS STORIES.

Attending Henry Ward Beecher's Church—What Lincoln said of Beecher.

Mr. Nelson Sizer, one of the gallery ushers of Henry Ward Beecher's church in Brooklyn, told a friend that about the time of the Cooper Institute speech, Mr. Lincoln was twice present at the morning services of that church. On the first occasion, he was accompanied by his friend, George B. Lincoln, Esq., and occupied a prominent seat in the centre of the house. On a subsequent Sunday morning, not long afterwards, the church was *packed*, as usual, and the services had proceeded to the announcement of the text, when the gallery door at the right of the organ-loft opened, and the tall figure of Mr. Lincoln entered, alone. Again in the city over Sunday, he started out by himself to find the church, which he reached considerably behind time. Every seat was occupied; but the gentle-manly usher at once surrendered his own, and, stepping back, became much interested in watching the effect of the sermon upon the western orator. As Mr. Beecher devel-oped his line of argument, Mr. Lincoln's body swayed for-ward, his lips parted, and he seemed at length entirely unconscious of his surroundings—frequently giving vent to his satisfaction, at a well-put point or illustration, with a kind of involuntary Indian exclamation — "*ugh!*"—not audible beyond his immediate presence, but *very* expressive! Mr. Lincoln henceforward had a profound admiration for the talents of the famous pastor of Plymouth Church. He once remarked to the Rev. Henry M. Field, of New York, that " he thought there was not upon record, in ancient or modern biography, so *productive* a mind, as had been exhibited in the career of Henry Ward Beecher ! "

Lincoln's Love for Little Tad.

No matter who was with the President, or how intently absorbed, his little son Tad was always welcome. He almost always accompanied his father. Once on the way to Fortress Monroe, he became very troublesome. The President was much engaged in conversation with the party who accompanied him, and he at length said:

" Tad, if you will be a good boy, and not disturb me any more till we get to Fortress Monroe, I will give you a dollar."

The hope of reward was effectual for a while in securing silence, but, boy-like, Tad soon forgot his promise, and was as noisy as ever. Upon reaching their destination, however, he said, very promptly, " Father, I want my dollar."

Mr. Lincoln turned to him with the inquiry: " Tad, do you think you have earned it ? "

" Yes," was the sturdy reply.

Mr. Lincoln looked at him half reproachfully for an instant, and then taking from his pocket-book a dollar note, he said: " Well, my son, at any rate, I will keep *my part of the bargain.*"

While paying a visit to Commodore Porter at Fortress Monroe, on one occasion, an incident occurred, subsequently related by Lieutenant Braine, one of the officers on board the flag-ship, to the Rev. Dr. Ewer, of New York. Noticing that the banks of the river were dotted with Spring blossoms, the President said, with the manner of one asking a special favor: " Commodore, Tad is very fond of flowers; —won't you let a couple of your men take a boat and go with him for an hour or two along shore, and gather a few? It will be a great gratification to him."

An Interesting Story—Lincoln at the Five Points' House of Industry in New York.

When Mr. Lincoln visited New York in 1860, he felt a great interest in many of the institutions for reforming criminals and saving the young from a life of crime. Among others, he visited, unattended, the Five Points' House of Industry, and the Superintendent of the Sabbath-school there gave the following account of the event:

" One Sunday morning, I saw a tall, remarkable-looking man enter the room and take a seat among us. He listened with fixed attention to our exercises, and his countenance expressed such genuine interest that I approached him and suggested that he might be willing to say something to the children. He accepted the invitation with evident pleasure; and, coming forward, began a simple address, which at once fascinated every little hearer and hushed the room into silence. His language was strikingly beautiful, and his tones musical with intense feeling. The little faces would droop into sad conviction as he uttered sentences of warning, and would brighten into sunshine as he spoke cheerful words of promise. Once or twice he attempted to close his remarks, but the imperative shout of 'Go on! Oh, do go on!' would compel him to resume.

As I looked upon the gaunt and sinewy frame of the stranger, and marked his powerful head and determined features, now touched into softness by the impressions of the moment, I felt an irrepressible curiosity to learn something more about him, and while he was quietly leaving the room I begged to know his name. He courteously replied: 'It is Abraham Lincoln, from Illinois.' "

11

Lincoln and His New Hat.

Mr. G. B. Lincoln tells of an amusing circumstance which took place at Springfield soon after Mr. Lincoln's nomination in 1860. A hatter in Brooklyn secretly obtained the size of the future President's head, and made for him a very elegant hat, which he sent by his townsman, Lincoln, to Springfield. About the time it was presented, various other testimonials of a similar character had come in from different sections. Mr. Lincoln took the hat, and after admiring its texture and workmanship, put it on his head and walked up to a looking-glass. Glancing from the reflection to Mrs. Lincoln, he said, with his peculiar twinkle of the eye, "Well, wife, there is one thing likely to come out of this scrape, any how. We are going to have some *new clothes!*"

Lincoln's Feat at the Washington Navy Yard With an Axe.

One afternoon during the Summer of 1862, the President accompanied several gentlemen to the Washington Navy Yard, to witness some experiments with a newly-invented gun. Subsequently the party went aboard of one of the steamers lying at the wharf. A discussion was going on as to the merits of the invention, in the midst of which Mr. Lincoln caught sight of some *axes* hanging up outside of the cabin. Leaving the group, he quietly went forward, and taking one down, returned with it, and said:

"Gentlemen, you may talk about your ' Raphael repeaters ' and ' eleven-inch Dahlgrens;' but *here* is an institution which I guess I understand better than either of you." With that he held the axe out at arm's length by the end of the handle, or "helve," as the wood-cutters call it—a feat not another person of the party could perform, though all made the attempt.

In such acts as this, showing that he neither forgot nor was ashamed of his humble origin, the good President exhibited his true nobility of character. He was a perfect illustration of his favorite poet's words :

" The rank is but the guinea's stamp,
The man's the gold, for a' that!"

Lincoln's Failure as a Merchant—He, However, Six Years Later Pays the "National Debt."

It is interesting to recall the fact that at one time Mr. Lincoln seriously took into consideration the project of learning the blacksmith's trade. He was without means, and felt the immediate necessity of undertaking some business that would give him bread. It was while he was entertaining this project that an event occurred which, in his undeterminded state of mind, seemed to open a way to success in another quarter.

A man named Reuben Radford, the keeper of a small store in the Village of New Salem, had somehow incurred the displeasure of the Clary's Grove Boys, who had exercised their "regulating" prerogatives by irregularly breaking in his windows. William G. Greene, a friend of young Lincoln, riding by Radford's store soon afterward, was hailed by him, and told that he intended to sell out. Mr. Greene went into the store, and, looking around, offered him at random four hundred dollars for his stock. The offer was immediately accepted.

Lincoln happening in the next day, and being familiar with the value of the goods, Mr. Greene proposed to him to take an inventory of the stock, and see what sort of a bargain he had made. This he did, and it was found that the goods were worth six hundred dollars. Lincoln then made him an offer of a hundred and twenty-five dollars for his bargain, with the proposition that he and a man named Berry, as his partner, should take his (Greene's) place in the notes given to Radford. Mr. Greene agreed to the arrangement, but Radford declined it, except on condition that Greene would be their security, and this he at last assented to.

Berry proved to be a dissipated, trifling man, and the business soon became a wreck. Mr. Greene was obliged to go in and help Lincoln close it up, and not only do this but pay Radford's notes. All that young Lincoln won from the store was some very valuable experience, and the burden of a debt to Greene which, in conversations with the latter, he always spoke of as the *National debt*. But this national debt, unlike the majority of those which bear the title, was paid to the uttermost farthing in after years.

Six years afterwards, Mr. Greene, who knew nothing of the law in such cases, and had not troubled himself to inquire about it, and who had in the meantime removed to Tennessee, received notice from Mr. Lincoln that he was ready to pay him what he had paid for Berry—he (Lincoln) being legally bound to pay the liabilities of his partner.

Funeral Services of Lincoln's Mother—The Old Pastor and Young Abraham—A Remarkable Service.

Several months after the death of Lincoln's mother which occurred when he was but a few years old, child as he was, he wrote to Parson Elkin who had been their pastor when residing in Kentucky, begging him to come to Indiana, and preach her funeral sermon.

This was asking a great favor of their former minister, for it would require him to ride on horseback a hundred miles through the wilderness; and it is something to be re-

membered to the humble itinerant's honor that he was willing to pay this tribute of respect to the woman who had so
thoroughly honored him and his sacred office. He replied
to Abraham's invitation, that he would preach the sermon
on a certain future Sunday, and gave him liberty to notify
the neighbors of the promised service.

As the appointed day approached, notice was given to
the whole neighborhood, embracing every family within
twenty miles. Neighbor carried the notice to neighbor. It
was scattered from every little school. There was probably
not a family that did not receive intelligence of the anx-
iously-anticipated event.

On a bright Sabbath morning, the settlers of the region
started for the cabin of the Lincolns; and, as they gathered
in, they presented a picture worthy the pencil of the
worthiest painter. Some came in carts of the rudest con-
struction, their wheels consisting of sections of the huge
boles of forest trees, and every other member the product
of the axe and auger; some came on horseback, two or
three upon a horse; others came in wagons drawn by oxen,
and still others came on foot. Two hundred persons in all
were assembled when Parson Elkin came out from the Lincoln cabin, accompanied by the little family, and proceeded
to the tree under which the precious dust of a wife and
mother was buried.

The congregation, seated upon stumps and logs around
the grave, received the preacher and the mourning family
in a silence broken only by the songs of birds, and the mur-
mur of insects, or the creaking cart of some late comer.
Taking his stand at the foot of the grave, Parson Elkin
lifted his voice in prayer and sacred song, and then preached
a sermon.

The occasion, the eager faces around him, and all the
sweet influences of the morning, inspired him with an un-

usual fluency and fervor; and the flickering sunlight, as it glanced through the wind-parted leaves, caught many a tear upon the bronzed cheeks of his auditors, while father and son were overcome by the revival of their great grief. He spoke of the precious Christian woman who had gone with the warm praise which she deserved, and held her up as an example of true womanhood.

Those who knew the tender and reverent spirit of Abraham Lincoln later in life, will not doubt that he returned to his cabin-home deeply impressed by all that he had heard. It was the rounding up for him of the influences of a Christian mother's life and teachings. It recalled her sweet and patient example, her assiduous efforts to inspire him with pure and noble motives, her simple instructions in divine truth, her devoted love for him, and the motherly offices she had rendered him during all his tender years. His character was planted in this Christian mother's life. Its roots were fed by this Christian mother's love; and those that have wondered at the truthfulness and earnestness of his mature character, have only to remember that the tree was true to the soil from which it sprung.

Something Concerning Mr. Lincoln's Religious Views.

The Rev. Mr. Willets, of Brooklyn, gives an account of a conversation with Mr. Lincoln, on the part of a lady of his acquaintance, connected with the "Christian Commission," who in the prosecution of her duties had several interviews with him.

The President, it seemed, had been much impressed with the devotion and earnestness of purpose manifested by the lady, and on one occasion, after she had discharged the object of her visit, he said to her:

" Mrs. ——, I have formed a high opinion of your Christian character, and now, as we are alone, I have a mind to ask you to give me, in brief, your idea of what constitutes a true religious experience."

The lady replied at some length, stating that, in her judgment, it consisted of a conviction of one's own sinfulness and weakness, and personal need of the Saviour for strength and support; that views of mere doctrine might and would differ, but when one was really brought to feel his need of Divine help, and to seek the aid of the Holy Spirit for strength and guidance, it was satisfactory evidence of his having been born again. This was the substance of her reply.

When she had concluded, Mr. Lincoln was very thoughtful for a few moments. He at length said, very earnestly, "If what you have told me is really a correct view of this great subject, I think I can say with sincerity, that I hope I am a Christian. I had lived," he continued, "until my boy Willie died, without realizing fully these things. That blow overwhelmed me. It showed me my weakness as I had never felt it before, and if I can take what you have stated as a *test*, I think I can safely say that I know something of that *change* of which you speak; and I will further add, that it has been my intention for some time, at a suitable opportunity, to make a public religious profession."

Thurlow Weed's Recollections.

In a letter to the New York Lincoln Club, Thurlow Weed remarks: I went to the Whig National Convention, at Chicago, in 1860, warmly in favor of and confidently expecting the nomination of Governor Seward. That disappointment of long-cherished hopes was a bitter one. I then accepted, very reluctantly, an invitation to visit Mr. Lincoln at his residence in Springfield, where, in an interesting conversation, even while smarting under the sense of injustice to Mr. Seward, confidence in Mr. Lincoln's good sense, capacity and fidelity was inspired.

A campaign programme was agreed upon, and, returning to Albany, I went to work as zealously and as cheerfully as I should have done with Mr. Seward as our Presidential nominee. Mr. Lincoln's inauguration simultaneously inaugurated rebellion. Events soon proved that the Chicago Convention had been wisely if not providentially guided. The country in its greatest emergency had, what it so greatly needed, the services of two, instead of one, of its greatest and best men. With Lincoln as President and Seward as Secretary of State, the right men were in the right places.

With ample opportunities to study the character of Abraham Lincoln, I never hesitated in declaring that his sense of public and private duty and honor was as high and his patriotism as devoted as that of George Washington.

Their names and their memories should descend to future generations as examples worthy of imitation.

An Amusing Illustration.

One of Mr. Lincoln's illustrations given by him on one occasion was that of a man who, in driving the hoops of a hogshead to "head" it up, was much annoyed by the constant falling in of the top. At length the bright idea struck him of putting his little boy inside to "hold it up." This he did; it never occurring to him till the job was done, how he was to get his child out. "This," said Lincoln, "is a fair sample of the way *some people always do business.*"

A Couple of Good Stories—How Lincoln took His Altitude— A Prophetic Bowl of Milk.

Soon after Mr. Lincoln's nomination for the Presidency, the Executive Chamber, a large fine room in the State House at Springfield was set apart for him, where he met the public until after his election.

As illustrative of the nature of many of his calls, the following brace of incidents were related to Mr. Holland by an eye witness: " Mr. Lincoln, being seated in conversation with a gentleman one day, two raw, plainly-dressed young ' Suckers ' entered the room, and bashfully lingered near the door. As soon as he observed them, and apprehended their embarrassment, he rose and walked to them, saying, " How do you do, my good fellows ? What can I do for you ? Will you sit down ?" The spokesman of the pair, the shorter of the two, declined to sit, and explained the object of the call thus: he had had a talk about the relative height of Mr. Lincoln and his companion, and had asserted his belief that they were of exactly the same height. He had come in to verify his judgment. Mr. Lincoln smiled, went and got his cane, and, placing the end of it upon the wall, said:

"Here, young man, come under here."

The young man came under the cane, as Mr. Lincoln held it, and when it was perfectly adjusted to his height, Mr. Lincoln said:

" Now, come out, and hold up the cane."

This he did while Mr. Lincoln stepped under. Rubbing his head back and forth to see that it worked easily under the measurement, he stepped out, and declared to the sagacious fellow who was curiously looking on, that he had guessed with remarkable accuracy—that he and the young man were exactly of the same height. Then he shook hands with them and sent them on their way. Mr. Lincoln would just as soon have thought of cutting off his right hand as he would have thought of turning those boys away with the impression that they had in any way insulted his dignity.

They had hardly disappeared when an old and modestly-dressed woman made her appearance. She knew Mr. Lincoln, but Mr. Lincoln did not at first recognize her. Then she undertook to recall to his memory certain incidents connected with his rides upon the circuit—especially his dining at her house upon the road at different times. Then he remembered her and her home. Having fixed her own place in his recollection, she tried to recall to him a certain scanty dinner of bread and milk that he once ate at her house. He could not remember it—on the contrary, he only remembered that he had always fared well at her house.

" Well," said she, " one day you came along after we had got through dinner, and we had eaten up everything, and I could give you nothing but a bowl of bread and milk; and you ate it; and when you got up you said it was *good enough for the President of the United States!* "

The good woman had come in from the country making a journey of eight or ten miles, to relate to Mr. Lincoln this incident, which, in her mind, had doubtless taken the form of prophecy. Mr. Lincoln placed the honest creature at her ease, chatted with her of old times, and dismissed her in the most happy and complacent frame of mind.

Lincoln's Love for the Little Ones.

Soon after his election as President and while visiting Chicago, one evening at a social gathering Mr. Lincoln saw a little girl timidly approaching him. He at once called her to him, and asked the little girl what she wished.

She replied that she wanted his name.

ABRAHAM LINCOLN'S RESIDENCE AT SPRINGFIELD, ILL.

Mr. Lincoln looked back into the room and said: " But here are other little girls—they would feel badly if I should give my name only to you."

The little girl replied that there were eight of them in all.

" Then," said Mr. Lincoln, " get me eight sheets of paper, and a pen and ink, and I will see what I can do for you."

The paper was brought, and Mr. Lincoln sat down in the crowded drawing-room, and wrote a sentence upon each sheet, appending his name; and thus every little girl carried off her souvenir.

During the same visit and while giving a reception at one of the hotels, a fond father took in a little boy by the hand who was anxious to see the new President. The moment the child entered the parlor door he, of his own accord and quite to the surprise of his father, took off his hat, and, giving it a swing, cried: " Hurrah for Lincoln !" There was a crowd, but as soon as Mr. Lincoln could get hold of the little fellow, he lifted him in his hands, and, tossing him towards the ceiling, laughingly shouted: " Hurrah for you !"

It was evidently a refreshing incident to Lincoln in the dreary work of hand-shaking.

An Interesting Anecdote of Lincoln Related by Rev. J. P. Gulliver.

On the morning following Lincoln's speech, in Norwich, Conn., Mr. Gulliver met Mr. Lincoln upon a train of cars, and entered into conversation with him. In speaking of his speech, Mr. Gulliver remarked to Mr. Lincoln that he thought it the most remarkable one he ever heard.

" Are you sincere in what you say?" inquired Mr. Lincoln.

" I mean every word of it," replied the minister. " Indeed, sir," he continued, " I learned more of the art of public speaking last evening than I could from a whole course of lectures on rhetoric."

Then Mr. Lincoln informed him of " a most extraordinary circumstance " that occurred at New Haven a few days previously. A professor of rhetoric in Yale College, he had been told, came to hear him, took notes of his speech, and gave a lecture on it to his class the following day; and, not satisfied with that, followed him to Meriden the next evening, and heard him again for the same purpose. All this seemed to Mr. Lincoln to be " very extraordinary." He had been sufficiently astonished by his success at the the West, but he had no expectation of any marked success at the East, particularly among literary and learned men.

" Now," said Mr. Lincoln, " I should very much like to know what it was in my speech which you thought so remarkable, and which interested my friend the professor so much ? "

Mr. Gulliver's answer was, " The clearness of your statements, the unanswerable style of your reasoning, and, especially, your illustrations, which were romance and pathos and fun and logic all welded together."

After Mr. Gulliver had fully satisfied his curiosity by a further exposition of the politician's peculiar power, Mr. Lincoln said:

" I am much obliged to you for this. I have been wishing for a long time to find some one who would make this analysis for me. It throws light on a subject which has been dark to me. I can understand very readily how such a power as you have ascribed to me will account for the effect which seems to be produced by my speeches. I hope you have not been too flattering in your estimate. Certainly, I have had a most wonderful success for a man of my limited education."

A Lincoln Story about Little Dan Webster's Soiled Hands!—How Dan Escaped a Flogging.

Mr. Lincoln, on one occasion narrated to Hon. Mr. Odell and others, with much zest, the following story about young Daniel Webster :

When quite young, at school, Daniel was one day guilty of a gross violation of the rules. He was detected in the act, and called up by the teacher for punishment. This was to be the old-fashioned "feruling" of the hand. His hands happended to be very dirty. Knowing this, on his way to the teacher's desk, he *spit* upon the palm of his *right* hand, wiping it off upon the side of his pantaloons.

"Give me your hand, sir," said the teacher, very sternly.

Out went the right hand, partly cleansed. The teacher looked at it a moment, and said:

"Daniel! if you will find another hand in this school-room as filthy as that, I will let you off this time!"

Instantly from behind his back came the *left* hand. "Here it is, sir," was the ready reply.

"That will do," said the teacher, "for this time; you can take your seat, sir."

Lincoln and the Little Baby—A Touching Story.

"Old Daniel," who was one of the White House ushers, is responsible for the following touching story:

A poor woman from Philadelphia had been waiting with a baby in her arms for several days to see the President. It appeared by her story, that her husband had furnished a substitute for the army, but sometime afterward, in a state of intoxication, was induced to enlist. Upon reaching the post assigned his regiment, he deserted, thinking the government was not entitled to his services. Returning home, he was arrested, tried, convicted, and sentenced to be shot.

The sentence was to be executed on a Saturday. On Monday his wife left her home with her baby, to endeavor to see the President.

Said Daniel, " She had been waiting here three days, and there was no chance for her to get in. Late in the afternoon of the third day, the President was going through the passage to his private room to get a cup of tea. On the way he heard the baby cry. He instantly went back to his office and rang the bell.

" Daniel," said he, " is there a woman with a baby in the ante-room?"

I said there was, and if he would allow me to say it, it was a case he ought to see; for it was a matter of life and death.

Said he, " Send her to me at once."

She went in, told her story, and the President pardoned her husband.

As the woman came out from his presence, her eyes were lifted and her lips moving in prayer, the tears streaming down her cheeks."

Said Daniel, " I went up to her, and pulling her shawl, said, ' Madam, it was the *baby that did it.*' "

D. L. Moody's Story of Lincoln's Compassion—What a Little Girl Did with Mr. Lincoln to Save Her Brother.

During the war, says D. L. Moody, I remember a young man, not twenty, who was court-martialed at the front and sentenced to be shot. The story was this: The young fellow had enlisted. He was not obliged to, but he went off with another young man. They were what we would call "chums." One night his companion was ordered out on picket duty, and he asked the young man to go for him. The next night he was ordered out himself; and having been awake two nights, and not being used to it, fell asleep at his post, and for the offense he was tried and sentenced to death. It was right after the order issued by the President that no interference would be allowed in cases of this kind. This sort of thing had become too frequent, and it must be stopped. When the news reached the father and mother in Vermont it nearly broke their hearts. The thought that their son should be shot was too great for them. They had no hope that he would be saved by anything they could do. But they had a little daughter who had read the life of Abraham Lincoln, and knew how he had loved his own children, and she said : " If Abraham Lincoln knew how my father and mother loved my brother he wouldn't let him be shot." That little girl thought this matter over and made up her mind to see the President. She went to the White House, and the sentinel, when he saw her imploring looks, passed her in, and when she came to the door and told the private secretary that she wanted to see the President, he could not refuse her. She came into the chamber and found Abraham Lincoln surrounded by his generals and counselors, and when he saw the little country girl he asked her what she wanted. The little maid told her plain, simple story—how her brother, whom her father and mother loved very dearly, had been sentenced to be shot ; how they were mourning for him, and if he was to die in that way it would break their hearts. The President's heart was touched with compassion, and he immediately sent a dispatch canceling the sentence and giving the boy a parole so that he could come home and see that father and mother. I just tell you this to show you how Abraham Lincoln's heart was moved by compassion for the sorrow of that father and mother, and if he showed so much do you think the Son of God will not have compassion upon you, sinner, if you only take that crushed, bruised heart to Him ?

12

Lincoln Joking Douglas—A Splendid "Whisky Cask."

On one occasion, when Lincoln and Douglas were "stumping" the State of Illinois together as political opponents, Douglas, who had the first speech, remarked that in early life, his father, who he said was an excellent cooper by trade, apprenticed him out to learn the cabinet business.

This was too good for Lincoln to let pass, so when his turn came to reply, he said :

"I had understood before that Mr. Douglas had been bound out to learn the cabinet-making business, which is all well enough, but I was not aware until now that his father was a cooper. I have no doubt, however, that he was one, and I am certain, also, that he was a very good one, for (here Lincoln gently bowed toward Douglas) he has made *one of the best whisky casks I have ever seen.*"

As Douglas was a short heavy-set man, and occasionally imbibed, the pith of the joke was at once apparent, and most heartily enjoyed by all.

On another occasion, Douglas in one of his speeches, made a strong point against Lincoln by telling the crowd that when he first knew Mr. Lincoln he was a "grocery-keeper," and sold whisky, cigars, etc. "Mr. L.," he said, "was a *very good bar-tender!*" This brought the laugh on Lincoln, whose reply, however, soon came, and then the laugh was on the other side.

"What Mr. Douglas has said, gentlemen," replied Mr. Lincoln, "is true enough; I did keep a grocery and I did sell cotton, candles and cigars, and sometimes whisky; but I remember in those days that Mr. Douglas was one of my *best customers!*

"Many a time have I stood on one side of the counter and sold whisky to Douglas on the other side, but the difference between us *now* is this: I have left my side of the counter, but Mr. Douglas *still sticks to his* as tenaciously as ever!"

Lincoln's Life as Written by Himself—The Whole Thing in a Nut Shell.

The compiler of the "Dictionary of Congress" states that while preparing that work for publication in 1858, he sent to Mr. Lincoln the usual request for a sketch of his life, and received the following reply :

"Born February 12, 1809, in Hardin County, Kentucky."

"Education Defective." "Profession a Lawyer" "Have been a Captain of Volunteers in Black Hawk War." "Postmaster at a very small office." "Four times a member of the Illinois Legislature, and was a member of the Lower House of Congress."　Yours, etc.

"A. LINCOLN."

How Lincoln Won a Case from his Partner—Laughable Toilet Ignorance.

While Judge Logan, of Springfield, Ill., was Lincoln's partner, two farmers, who had a misunderstanding respecting a horse trade, went to law.　By mutual consent the partners in law became antagonists in this case.　On the day of the trial Mr. Logan, having bought a new shirt, open in the back, with a huge standing collar, dressed himself in extreme haste, and put on the shirt with the bosom at the back, a linen coat concealing the blunder.　He dazed the jury with his knowledge of "horse points," and as the day was sultry, took off his coat and summed up in his shirt-sleeves.

Lincoln sitting behind him, took in the situation, and when his turn came, remarked to the jury:

"Gentlemen, Mr. Logan has been trying for over an hour to make you believe he knows more about a horse than these honest old farmers who are witnesses.　He has quoted largely from his 'horse doctor,' and now, gentlemen, I sub. mit to you, (here he lifted Logan out of his chair, and turned him with his back to the jury and the crowd, at the same time flipping up the enormous standing collar) what dependence can you place in his horse knowledge when he *has not sense enough to put on his shirt ?* "

The roars of laughter that greeted this exhibition, and the verdict that Lincoln got soon after, gave Logan a permanent prejudice against " bosom shirts."

Little Lincoln Stories.

An old Englishman who resided in Springfield, Ills., hearing the results of the Political Convention at Chicago, could not contain his astonishment. " What ! " said he, " Abe Lincoln nominated for President of the United States ? Can it be possible ! A man that buys a ten cent beef-steak for his breakfast, and carries it home himself! "

Mr. Lincoln being asked by a friend how he felt when the returns came in that insured his defeat, replied that " he felt, he supposed, very much like the stripling who had stumped his toe; too *badly* to *laugh* and too *big* to *cry.'*

A young man bred in Springfield speaks of a vision that has clung to his memory very vividly, of Mr. Lincoln as he appeared in those days. His way to school led by the lawyer's door. On almost any fair summer morning, he could find Mr. Lincoln on the sidewalk, in front of his house, drawing a child back and forth, in a baby carriage.

Mr. Lincoln never made his profession lucrative to himself. It was very difficult for him to charge a heavy fee to anybody, and still more difficult for him to charge his friends anything at all for professional services. To a poor client, he was quite as apt to give money as to take it from him. He never encouraged the spirit of litigation. Henry McHenry, one of his old clients, says that he went to Mr. Lincoln with a case to prosecute, and that Mr. Lincoln refused to have anything to do with it, because he was not strictly in the right. "You can give the other party a great deal of trouble," said the lawyer, "and perhaps beat him, but you had better let the suit alone."

FROM the original manuscript of one of Mr. Lincoln's speeches, these words are transferred: "Twenty-two years ago, Judge Douglas and I first became acquainted. We were both young then—he a trifle younger than I. Even then we were both ambitious,—I, perhaps, quite as much so as he. With me, the race of ambition has been a failure—a flat failure; with him, it has been one of splendid success. His name fills the nation, and is not unknown even in foreign lands. I affect no contempt for the high eminence he has reached. So reached that the oppressed of my species might have shared with me in the elevation, I would rather stand on that eminence than wear the richest crown that ever pressed a monarch's brow."

IN one of Lincoln's early speeches against slavery he said : "My distinguished friend (Stephen A. Douglas) says, it is an insult to the emigrants to Kansas and Nebraska to suppose they are not able to govern themselves. We must not slur over an argument of this kind because it happens to tickle the ear. It must be met and answered. I admit that the emigrant to Kansas and Nebraska is competent to govern himself, but (the speaker rising to his full height), *I deny his right to govern any other person without that person's consent.*" That touched the very marrow of the matter, and revealed the whole difference between Lincoln and Douglas.

Lincoln's Last Story and Last Written Words and Conversations.

The last story told by Mr. Lincoln was drawn out by a circumstance which occurred just before the interview with Messrs. Colfax and Ashmun, on the evening of his assassination.

Marshal Lamon, of Washington, had called upon him with an application for the pardon of a soldier. After a brief hearing the President took the application, and, when about to write his name upon the back of it, he looked up and said :

" Lamon, have you ever heard how the Patagonians eat oysters? They open them and throw the shells out of the window until the pile gets higher than the house, and then they move;" adding :

' I feel to-day like commencing a new pile of pardons, and I may as well begin it just here."

At the subsequent interview with Messrs. Colfax and Ashmun, Mr. Lincoln was in high spirits. The uneasiness felt by his friends during his visit to Richmond was dwelt upon, when he sportively replied that he "supposed he should have been uneasy also, had any other man been President and gone there; but as it was, he felt no apprehension of danger whatever." Turning to Speaker Colfax, he said :

"Sumner has the 'gavel' of the Confederate Congress, which he got at Richmond, and intended giving it to the Secretary of War, but I insisted he must give it to you, and you tell him from me to hand it over."

Mr. Ashmun, who was the presiding officer of the Chicago Convention in 1860, alluded to the " gavel " used on that occasion, saying he had preserved it as a valuable memento.

Mr. Ashmun then referred to a matter of business connected with a cotton claim, preferred by a client of his, and said that he desired to have a " commission " appointed to examine and decide upon the merits of the case.   Mr. Lincoln replied, with considerable warmth of manner, " I have done with ' commissions.'   I believe they are contrivances to *cheat* the Government out of every pound of cotton they can lay their hands on."   Mr. Ashmun's face flushed, and he replied that he hoped the President meant no personal imputation.

Mr. Lincoln saw that he had wounded his friend, and he instantly replied: " You did not understand me, Ashmun. I did not mean what you inferred.   I take it all back." Subsequently he said: " I apologize to you, Ashmun."

He then engaged to see Mr. Ashmun early the next morning, and, taking a card, he wrote:

" Allow Mr. Ashmun and friend to come in at 9 A. M. to-morrow.

A. LINCOLN."

These were his last written words.   Turning to Mr. Colfax he said: " You will accompany Mrs. Lincoln and me to the theatre, I hope?"   Mr. Colfax pleaded other engagements—expecting to start on his Pacific trip the next morning.   The party passed out on the portico together, the President saying at the very last:

" Colfax, don't forget to tell the people of the mining regions what I told you this morning about the development when peace comes;" then shaking hands with both gentlemen, he followed Mrs. Lincoln into the carriage, leaning forward, at the last moment, to say as they were driven off, " I will telegraph you, Colfax, at San Francisco,"— passing thus forth for the last time from under that roof into the creeping shadows which were to settle before another dawn into a funeral pall upon the orphaned heart of the nation.

**Abraham Lincoln's Death—Walt Whitman's Vivid Description of
the Scene at Ford's Theatre.**

The day (April 14, 1865,) seems to have been a pleasant
one throughout the whole land—the moral atmosphere
pleasant, too—the long storm, so dark, so fratricidal, full of
blood and doubt and gloom, over and ended at last by the
sunrise of such an absolute National victory, and utter
breaking down of secessionism—we almost doubted our
senses! Lee had capitulated beneath the apple tree at
Appommatox. The other armies, the flanges of the revolt,
swiftly followed.

And could it really be, then? Out of all the affairs of
this world of woe and passion, of failure and disorder and
dismay, was there really come the confirmed, unerring sign
of peace, like a shaft of pure light—of rightful rule—of
God?

But I must not dwell on accessories. The deed hastens.
The popular afternoon paper, the little *Evening Star*, had
scattered all over its third page, divided among the adver-
tisements in a sensational manner in a hundred different
places: " The President and his lady will be at the theatre
this evening." Lincoln was fond of the theatre. I have
myself seen him there several times. I remember thinking
how funny it was that he, in some respects the leading
actor in the greatest and stormiest drama known to real
history's stage, through centuries, should sit there and be
so completely interested in those human jack-straws, moving
about with their silly little gestures, foreign spirit, and flat-
ulent text.

So the day, as I say, was propitious. Early herbage,
early flowers, were out. I remember where I was stopping
at the time, the season being advanced, there were many
lilacs in full bloom. By one of those caprices that enter
and give tinge to events without being at all a part of them,

I find myself always reminded of the great tragedy of that day by the sight and odor of these blossoms. It never fails.

On this occasion the theatre was crowded, many ladies in rich and gay costumes, officers in their uniforms, many well-known citizens, young folks, the usual clusters of gas, lights, the usual magnetism of so many people, cheerful, with perfumes, music of violins and flutes—and over all, and saturating, that vast, vague wonder, Victory, the Nation's victory, the triumph of the Union, filling the air, the thought, the sense, with exhilaration more than all perfumes.

The President came betimes, and, with his wife, witnessed the play, from the large stage boxes of the second tier, two thrown into one, and profusely draped with the National flag. The acts and scenes of the piece—one of those singularly witless compositions which have at least the merit of giving entire relief to an audience engaged in mental action or business excitements and cares during the day, as it makes not the slightest call on cither the moral, emotional, esthetic or spiritual nature—a piece (" Our American Cousin ") in which, among other characters so called, a Yankee, certainly such a one as was never seen, or at least like it ever seen in North America, is introduced in England, with a varied fol-de-rol of talk, plot, scenery, and such phantasmagoria as goes to make up a modern popular drama—had progressed through perhaps a couple of its acts, when in the midst of this comedy, or tragedy, or non-such, or whatever it is to be called, and to offset it, or finish it out, as if in Nature's and the Great Muse's mockery of these poor mimies, comes interpolated that scene, not really or exactly to be described at all (for on the many hundreds who were there it seems to this hour to have left little but a passing blur, a dream, a blotch)—and yet partially to be described as I now proceed to give it:

There is a scene in the play representing the modern parlor, in which two unprecedented English ladies are informed by the unprecedented and impossible Yankee that he is not a man of fortune, and therefore undesirable for marriage catching purposes; after which, the comments being finished, the dramatic trio make exit, leaving the stage clear for a moment. There was a pause, a hush, as it were. At this period came the murder of Abraham Lincoln. Great as that was, with all its manifold train circling around it, and stretching into the future for many a century, in the politics, history, art, etc., of the New World, in point of fact, the main thing, the actual murder, transpired with the quiet and simplicity of any commonest occurrence—the bursting of a bud or pod in the growth of vegetation, for instance.

Through the general hum following the stage pause, with the change of positions, etc., came the muffled sound of a pistol shot, which not one-hundredth part of the audience heard at the time—and yet a moment's hush—somehow, surely a vague, startled thrill—and then, through the ornamented, draperied, starred, and striped space-way of the President's box, a sudden figure, a man, raises himself with hands and feet, stands a moment on the railing, leaps below to the stage (a distance of perhaps of 14 or 15 feet), falls out of position catching his boot-heel in the copious drapery (the American flag), falls on one knee, quickly recovers himself, rises as if nothing had happened (he really sprains his ankle, but unfelt then)—and the figure, Booth, the murderer, dressed in plain black broadcloth, bare-headed, with a full head of glossy, raven hair, and his eyes, like some mad animal's flashing with light and resolution, yet with a certain strange calmness, holds aloft in one hand a large knife—walks along not much back of the foot-lights —turns fully towards the audience his face of statuesque beauty, lit by those basilisk eyes, flashing with desperation, perhaps insanity—launches out in a firm and steady voice the words *Sic Semper Tyrannis*—and then walks with neither slow nor very rapid pace diagonally across to the back of the stage, and disappears. (Had not all this terrible scene—making the mimic ones preposterous—had it not all been rehearsed, in blank, by Booth, beforehand?)

A moment's hush, incredulous—a scream—the cry of murder—Mrs. Lincoln leaning out of the box, with ashy cheeks and lips, with involuntary cry, pointing to the retreating figure, " He has killed the President." And still a moment's strange, incredulous suspense—and then the deluge!—then that mixture of horror, noises, uncertainty—(the sound, somewhere back, of a horse's hoofs clattering with speed) the people burst through chairs and railings, and break them up—that noise adds to the queerness of the scene—there is extricable confusion and terror—women faint—quite feeble persons fall, and are trampled on—many cries of agony are heard—the broad stage suddenly fills to suffocation with a dense and motley crowd, like some horrible carnival—the audience rush generally upon it—at least the strong men do—the actors and actresses are there in their play costumes and painted faces, with moral fright showing through the rouge—some trembling, some in tears the screams and calls, confused talk—redoubled, trebled— two or three manage to pass up water from the stage to the President's box—others try to clamber up—etc., etc.

In the midst of all this the soldiers of the President's Guard, with others, suddenly drawn to the scene, burst in —some 200 altogether—they storm the house, through all the tiers, especially the upper ones—inflamed with fury, literally charging the audience with fixed bayonets, muskets and pistols, shouting " Clear out! clear out!—you sons of b—!" Such the wild scene, or a suggestion of it rather, inside the play house that night.

Outside, too, in the atmosphere of shock and craze, crowds of people, filled with frenzy, ready to seize any outlet for it, came near committing murder several times on innocent individuals. One such case was especially exciting. The infuriated crowd, through some chance, got started against one man, either for words he uttered, or perhaps without any cause at all, and were proceeding at once to hang him on a neighboring lamp-post, when he was rescued by a few heroic policemen, who placed him in their midst and fought their way slowly and amid great peril toward the station house. It was a fitting episode of the whole affair. The crowd rushing and eddying to and fro—the night, the yells, the pale faces, many frightened people trying in vain to extricate themselves—the attacked man, not yet freed from the jaws of death, looking like a corpse—the silent, resolute half dozen policemen, with no weapons but their little clubs, yet stern and steady through all those eddying swarms—made indeed a fitting side scene to the grand tragedy of the murder. They gained the station house with the protected man, whom they placed in security for the night, and discharged him in the morning.

And in the midst of that night pandemonium of senseless hate, infuriated soldiers, the audience and the crowd—the stage, and all its actors and actresses, its paint pots, spangles and gaslight—the life blood from those veins, the best and sweetest of the land, drips slowly down, and death's ooze already begins its little bubbles on the lips.

Such, hurriedly sketched, were the accompaniments of the death of President Lincoln. So suddenly, and in murder and horror unsurpassed, he was taken from us. But his death was painless.

GETTING AT THE PASS-WORD.

An amusing story is attributed to the late President Lincoln about the Iowa First, and the changes which a certain pass-word underwent about the time of the battle of Springfield. One of the Dubuque officers, whose duty it was to furnish the guards with a pass-word for the night, gave the word "Potomac." A German on guard, not comprehending distinctly the difference between B's and P's, understood it to be "Bottomic," and this, on being transferred to another, was corrupted into "Buttermilk." Soon afterwards the officer who had given the word wished to return through the lines, and on approaching a sentinel was ordered to halt, and the word demanded. He gave the word "Potomac." "Nicht right; you don't pass mit me dis way." "But this is the word, and I will pass." "No, you stan'," at the same time placing a bayonet at his breast, in a manner that told the officer that "Potomac" didn't pass in Missouri. "What is the word, then?" "Buttermilk." "Well, then, buttermilk." "Dat is right; now you pass mit yourself all about your piziness." There was then a general overhauling of the pass-word, and the difference between Potomac and Buttermilk being understood, the joke became one of the laughable incidents of the campaign.

STOP THE BOAT.

During the recent civil war a farmer from one of the border counties of Virginia appealed to President Lincoln to redress some small grievance which he had suffered at the hands of Union soldiers. The President replied that if he were to deal with such cases he should find work enough for twenty presidents. The farmer, however, urged his case, saying, "Couldn't you just give me a line to Col. —— about it? just one line!" "Ha, ha!" responded the President, "that reminds me of old Jack Chase. Jack used to be lumberman on the Illinois, and he was steady and sober, and the best raftsman on the river. It was quite a trick, twenty-five years ago, to take logs over the rapids, but he was skillful with a raft and always kept her straight in the channel. Finally a steamer was put on, and Jack was made captain of her. He always used to take the wheel, going through the rapids. One day when the boat was plunging and wallowing along the boiling current, and Jack's utmost vigilance was being exercised to keep her in the narrow channel, a boy pulled his coat-tail and hailed him with: 'Say, Mr. Captain! I wish you would just stop your boat a minute—I've lost my apple overboard!'"

Lincoln and a Clergyman.

At the semi-annual meeting of the New Jersey Historical Society, held in Newark, N. J., Rev. Dr. Sheldon, of Princeton, read a memorial of their late President, Rev. R. K. Rodgers, D. D., in which appears the following incident concerning Mr. Lincoln, and the war:

One day during the war, Dr. Rodgers was called on by a man in his congregation, who, in the greatest distress, told him that his son, a soldier in army, had just been sentenced to be shot for desertion, and begged the minister's interposition.

The Doctor went to Washington with the wife and infant child of the condemned man, and sent his card up to Mr. Lincoln. When admitted, the President said:

"You are a minister, I believe. What can I do for you, my friend?"

The reply was: 'A young man from my congregation in the army has so far forgotton his duty to his country and his God as to desert his colors, and is sentenced to die. I have come to ask you to spare him.'

With characteristic quaintness the President replied: 'Then you don't want him hurt, do you?'

'Oh, no,' said the petitioner, I did not mean that; he deserves punishment, but I beg for him time to prepare to meet his God.'

'Do you say he has father, wife and child?' said Mr. Lincoln.

'Yes.'

'Where do you say he is?'

On being told, he turned to his secretary, said a few words in an undertone, of which that official made note, and added to Dr. Rodgers, 'You have your request. Tell his friends I have reprieved him.'

With a 'God bless you Mr. President,' Dr. Rodgers turned away to bear the glad news to the distressed family."

The President Advises Secretary Stanton to Prepare for Death.

The imperious Stanton, when Secretary of War, took a fancy one day to a house in Washington that Lamon had just bargained for. He ordered the latter to vacate instanter. Lamon not only did not vacate, but went to Stanton and said he would kill him if he interfered with the house. Stanton was furious at the threat, and made it known at once to Lincoln. The latter said to the astonished War Secretary:

"Well, Stanton, if Ward has said he will kill you, he certainly will, and I'd advise you to prepare for death without further delay.

The President promised, however, to do what he could to appease the murderous Marshal, and this was the end of Stanton's attempt on the house.

"A Great Deal of Shuck for a Little Nubbin."

At the peace conference which occurred in February, 1865, at Fortres Monroe, President Lincoln and Secretary Seward were on one side, and Alexander H. Stephens, John A. Campbell and R. M. T. Hunter on the other. The attenuation of Mr. Stephens has so long been a matter of such general notoriety that it is not offensive to speak of it. It seems that Mr. Lincoln had never seen Mr. Stephens before. At that time a kind of cloth was worn by southern gentlemen, nearly the shade of ordinary corn husk, and Mr. Stephens' great coat was made of that material. But Mr. Stephens, who always had been a frail man, wore many other garments beneath to protect him against the raw wind of Hampton Roads; and Mr. Lincoln watched with much interest the process of shedding until the man was finally reached. At last Mr. Stephens stood forth in his physical entity, ready for business. Mr. Lincoln, giving Gov. Seward one of his most comical looks, and pointing to the discarded coats, said: "Well, I never saw as much shuck for as little a nubbin in my life."

How a Negro Soldier Argued the "Point."

The following story is attributed to Mr. Lincoln:

Upon the hurricane deck of one of our gunboats, an

elderly darkey with a very philosopical and retrospective cast of countenance, squatted upon his bundle, toasting his shins against the chimney, and apparently plunged into a state of profound meditation Finding, upon inquiry, that he belonged to the Ninth Illinois, one of the most gallantly behaved and heavy losing regiments at the Fort Donelson battle, and a part of which was aboard, I began to interrogate him on the subject:

"Were you in the fight?"

"Had a little taste of it sa."

"Stood your ground, did you?"

"No sa; I runs."

"Run at the first fire, did you?"

"Yes sa; and would hab run soona had I knowd it war coming."

"Why, that wasn't very creditable to your courage."

"Dat isn't my line, sa; cooking's my perfeshun."

"Well, but have you no regard for your reputation?"

"Reputation's nuffin to me by de side ob life."

"Do you consider your life worth more than other people's?"

"It is worth more to me, sa."

"Then you must value it very highly?"

"Yes, sa, I does; more dan all dis wuld, more dan a million ob dollars, sa; for what wud dat be wuth to a man wid de bref out of him? Self-preserbation am de fust law wid me."

"But why should you act upon a different rule from other men?"

"Because different men set different values upon their lives; mine is not in de market."

"But if you lost it, you would have the satisfaction of knowing that you died for your country."

"What satisfaction would dat be to me when de power ob feelin' was gone?"

"Then patriotism and honor are nothing to you?"

"Nuffin whatever, sa; I regard them as among the vanities."

"If our soldiers were like you, traitors might have broken up the government without resistance."

"Yes, sa; dar would hab been no help for it. I wouldn't put my life in de scale 'ginst any gobernment dat eber existed, for no gobernment could replace de loss to me."

"Do you think any of your company would have missed you if you had been killed?"

"Maybe not, sa; a dead white man ain't much to dese sogers, let alone a dead nigga; but I'd a missed myself and dat was de pint wid me."

The Boy Lincoln—How He Rode a Cow.

A writer in the Louisville *Courier-Journal*, gives the following interesting reminiscence of the "Boy Lincoln:"

"Lincoln's early youth was spent in Spencer county, Indiana, above Rockport, a beautiful little city crowning the abrupt cliffs which frown over the Ohio river. He was faithful and industrious, but there was in him a latent indolence which made him fond of taking his rod to fish, or, with his gun upon his shoulder, he would roam in search of game over the long, low hills bursting with red day. There are living at present several old citizens who knew Lincoln well at that time. He was thoughtful, and his solitary expeditions probably gave him plenty of opportunity to indulge his meditative faculties.

The description of his appearance then; his long, lank legs under an awkward body; his homely face upon which the prominent nose stood like a handle; his long hair dangling upon his shoulders, bring up instantly the picture of Ichapod Crane in the twilight stealing over the hills of Sleepy Hollow to pay his court to Fraulein Katrina Von Tassel.

The embryo statesman was full of spirit and fond of mad pranks.

One old gentleman in Rockport lives to tell of the last time he saw Lincoln. He was visiting the Lincoln homestead, and as he was coming away they found a trespassing cow hanging about the gate. The cow had given the Lincolns much annoyance by entering their garden and committing depredations. Young Abe was dressed in a suit of jeans, without any coat, as it was summer time, and on his head he wore a broad-brimed white straw hat, part of which was cracked and broken. Finding the cow standing hypocritically meek at the gate, young Abe leaped astride of her back, and, digging his bare heels into her sides, the astonished animal broke away down the road in a lumbering gallop. "The last I saw of Abe Lincoln," the old gentleman relates fondly, "he was swinging his hat, shouting at the top of his voice, galloping down the road on that thunderstruck cow."

In the old country church near the Lincoln place is a pulpit which was made by Abe Lincoln and his father. There is a bookcase in the Evansville Custom-House made by the same carpenters and taken there for preservation. Near where the old house stood is a dilapidated corn-crib with rail floor, the rails for which were split by young Lincoln. A monument has been raised over Nancy Lincoln's grave through the efforts of Gen. Veatch, of Rockport. It is a plain slab with a plain inscription.

An Inauguration Incident.

Noah Brooks, in his "Reminicences," relates the following incident: While the ceremonies of the second inauguration were in progress, just as Lincoln stepped forward to take the oath of office, the sun, which had been obscuredby rain-clouds, burst forth in splendor. In conversation, next day, the President asked, "Did you notice that sunburst? It made my heart jump." Later in the month, Miss Anna Dickinson, in a lecture delivered in the hall of the House of Representatives, eloquently alluded to the sunburst as a happy omen. The President sat directly in front of the speaker, and from the reporters' gallery, behind her, I had caught his eye, soon after he sat down. When Miss Dickinson referred to the sunbeam, he looked up to me, involuntarily, and I thought his eyes were suffused with moisture. Perhaps they were; but the next day he said, "I wonder if Miss Dickinson saw me wink at you?"

The Brigadier Generals and the Horses.

When President Lincoln heard of the rebel raid at Fairfax, in which a brigadier-general and a number of valuable horses were captured, he gravely observed, "Well I am sorry for the horses." "Sorry for the horses, Mr. President!" exclaimed the Secretary of War, raising his spectacles, and throwing himself back in his chair in astonishment. " Yes," replied Mr. Lincoln; " I can make a brigadier-general in five minutes, but it is not easy to replace a hundred and ten horses."

"Potomac," vs. " Buttermilk."

An amusing story is attributed to President Lincoln, about the Iowa First, and the changes which a certain password underwent about the time of the battle of Springfield.

One of the Dubuque officers, whose duty it was to furnish the guards with a pass-word lor the night, gave the word " Potomac." A German on guard, not comprehending distinctly the difference hetween B's and P's, understood it to be " Bottomic," and this, on being transferred to another, was corrupted into " Buttermilk." Soon afterward the officer who had given the word wished to return through the lines, and on approaching a sentinel was ordered to halt and the word demanded. He gave the word " Potomac."

" Nicht right; you don't pass mit me dis way."

" But this is the word, and I will pass."

" No, you stan'," at the same time placing a bayonet at his breast, in a manner that told the officer that 'Potomac' didn't pass in Missouri.

" What is the word, then?"

" Buttermilk."

" Well, then, buttermilk."

" Dat is right; you pass mit yourself all about your piziness."

There was then a general overhauling of the pass-word and the difference between Potomac and Buttermilk being understood, the joke became one of the laughable incidents of the campaign.

Lincoln's Own Humble Opinion of Himself—A Story Told by Judge Carter.

The following interesting story is from the "Note Book of Reminiscences" of Judge A. G. W. Carter:

The Republicans of Cincinnati in the year 1859 invited plain Abraham Lincoln, of Illinois, to that city to make a political speech in reply to one that had been made there a short time before by Stephen A. Douglas. This was some time after the famous campaigns of Lincoln and Douglas in the State of Illinois and by which both acquired and maintained so great a National reputation, which Lincoln never had before, but the reputation of Douglas had long since become National from his career in the United States Senate. Douglas had been there, and had made a very great Democratic speech, and the Republicans thought it quite necessary that the great effect of it should be modified and ameliorated by a speech from his own home rival, Mr. Lincoln.

So Lincoln was invited, and he came, arriving on the early evening of September 17, 1859, and he was duly escorted to his well prepared quarters at the Burnet House by a Republican committee. At half-past 7 o'clock a long procession, headed by Menter's famous brass band, reached the Burnet House, and there taking Mr. Lincoln along with them, marched to the Fifth street market space, and there, from the balcony of Mr. Kinsey's house, above his store, Mr. Lincoln made one of the best political speeches of his life to the immense concourse of his fellow citizens assembled to hear him for the first time.

I was living at the Burnet House at the time and Gov. Thomas Corwin had been living there for several months, and he proposed to me to accompany him up to the meeting to hear enough of Lincoln's speech to get the tenor and run of it, so that we might be enabled to talk about it with the orator after it was all over, for Mr. Corwin had arranged for Mr. Lincoln to spend a good portion of the night with him in his own room at the Burnet House, and had personally invited me to be one of the company. I went with Mr. Corwin, and standing on the market space with the rest of the multitude, we listened with great interest to Mr. Lincoln from the beginning to the end of his eloquent and thoroughly practical speech, for we could not get away from his eloquence. The night was calm and beautiful, the atmosphere balmy and delightful, and the clear, loud, penetrating tones of old Abe's voice, (for he was called " Old Abe " even then) reached to all points of the extended market place, and any one there could plainly and distinctly hear everything he said. I full remember the modest and humble beginning of his great speech:

" Fellow-citizens, " said he, in a very sincere manner and plain tone of voice, " this is the first time I ever undertook to speak to the people inhabiting so large a city, and I am not in the habit of making speeches in so large a city, and therefore I hope I will be excused for any errors or blunders that I may make before so large a meeting. "

This was truly a humble beginning, and the very simplicity and homespun manner and method of his exordium commanded at once the attention of the people, and for full two hours that vast concourse listened to him without interruption, save by their own applause. After he was through, Mr. Corwin, being seen in the crowd, was called for, but he did not make a speech on account of the lateness of the hour. He properly excused himself. Mr. Corwin and myself wended our way back to the Burnet House, and waited the arrival of Mr. Lincoln in the office, and after his friends and admirers had left him and the Burnet House, we approached him, and, by his invitation, accompanied him to his private room, No. 15, on the first floor adjoining the large hall of the office, and took seats with him. It was now about 11 o'clock at night, but Mr. Lincoln showed no signs of exhaustion or fatigue; on the contrary, he was lively and cheerful, and full of talk and fun. He sat in his chair with his feet and long legs upon and over the centre-table, and he began to tell his dry stories, in his dry way, and kept Mr. Corwin and myself for several hours in entertainment and hilarity.

I had heard of Mr. Lincoln as a story-teller, but I never knew that he was such a serious, sincere, earnest, funny one as he proved himself to be that night. He beat Corwin all hollow, and Mr. Corwin remarked to me that he would yield the palm of story-telling to Mr. Lincoln. But our interview was not all story-telling.

There was a good deal of serious political talk and philosophical reflection, and some personal talk, and of this last I desire to take particular notice, as manifesting in a marked degree the thorough simplicity, humility and modesty of the character of Abraham Lincoln.

"Well, Mr. Lincoln," said Mr. Corwin, "the people begin seriously to talk about you as a candidate for the Presidency."

Lincoln—"Oh, that is all talk of some enthusiastic

friends of mine in Illinois. There is nothing in it Mr. Corwin, there is nothing in it."

Mr. Corwin—"Oh! but there is. The talk is not confined to the State of Illinois, but it is all over the country. You have enthusiastic friends all over the country who are talking of you for the Presidency."

Lincoln—"Oh, the talk is not serious at all; it is just an enthusiastic impulse, and I don't mind it."

Corwin—"But it is serious, and as the convention of the Republicans will assemble early next year, it is the purpose to place your name before the convention for the Presidency, and they will perhaps nominate you."

Lincoln—"What! nominate me, when there are such great men as Seward and Chase in the field?"

Corwin—"There is the very point; the friends of Chase and Seward are already up in arms against each other, and who so fit to come in and reconcile all the interests and antagonisms of the contending friends and of these candidates?"

Lincoln—"So you really think there is a chance for *me?* Well, Mr. Corwin, I don't think there is any thing in it, and the fact is, I don't encourage the idea, and shall not encourage the idea, for I have no ambition to be President. That never entered my head. Indeed, Mr. Corwin, I do not think I am fit to be President of these United States. I have not the requisite ability. I am not competent to fill the Presidency. I cannot compare in anything with Chase and Seward. Now, I'll tell you what —I am willing to run for Vice-President, if the convention will nominate me for that, and with a little study of Cushing's or Jefferson's Manual I might acquire enough knowledge to sit in the chair of the Vice-President and preside over the deliberations of the Senate. You know it does not require a great genius to do that, and this I think I could be capable of with a little extra study."

Corwin—"But the people do not think so. They will want you for President."

Lincoln—"I don't think the people will be so foolish as that, Mr. Corwin, for I know that I am not fit to be President, and I know that the people know that, too. But I would really thank them and be very grateful to them if they would take it into their heads to make me their Vice-President, the duties of which, I believe, I could inform myself of to attend to. But I do not think at all of being President of this great county—no, not at all."

And so the conversation in this strain went on till 2 o'clock in the morning, but Lincoln stuck to it to the last that he was not fit to be President.

Mr. Corwin and myself bid good-bye to Mr. Lincoln in the wee hours of morn, that he might go to bed and to his proper sleep. As we came out of the room into the still open office, Mr. Corwin remarked to me sort o' confidentially, "A great man, that Abraham Lincoln, Judge Carter; so great, indeed, that he does not know anything about it himself. He will do for a President, he will make a first-rate one, and I think the Republican convention will nominate him fresh from the people, and the Republican people will elect him."

This was saying a great deal for Mr. Corwin, who was frequently talked of for President himself, and if he had followed his young career and successes might have been the President, but he got soured once upon a time, and he was no longer ambitious.

As to Mr. Lincoln, I think the recollection is too good

to be lost. It shows without a doubt the native simplicity and humility of the man, and he who has these in his soul as virtues, it is safe to say, has all the rest.

How Lincoln Told a Secret.

When the Sherman expedition which captured Port Royal went out, there was great curiosity to know where it had gone. A person visiting President Lincoln at his official residence importuned him to disclose the destinanation.

" Will you keep it entirely secret?" asked the President.

"Oh yes, upon my honor."

" Well, " said the President, " I'll tell you. " Assuming an air of great mystery, and drawing the man close to him, he kept him a moment awaiting the revelation with an open mouth and in great anxiety, and then said in a loud whisper, which was heard all over the room, " The expedition has gone to—sea. "

A Joke on Mr. Chase.

One day, while the American war was going on, and Secretary Chase was issuing the paper money, known as " greenbacks, " in large quantities, he found upon a desk in his office a drawing of an ingenious invention for turning gold eagles into " greenbacks, " with a portrait of himself feeding it with " yeller boys, " at one end, while the government currency came out at the other end, flying about like leaves of Autumn. While he was examining the drawing, President Lincoln came in, and, recognizing the likeness of the secretary, exclaimed:

"Capital joke, isn't it, Mr. Chase?"

"A joke," said the irate financier, " I'd give a thousand dollars to know who left that here. "

" Would you, indeed?" said the President, "and which end would you pay from?"

The answer is not "recorded."

A Curious Story of Lincoln and the Spirits—A "Seance."

It is stated on the authority of the Boston *Evening Gazette*, that Abraham Lincoln once gave a Spiritual *soiree* at the Presidential residence to test the wonderful alleged supernatural powers of one Mr. Charles E. Shockle. The party consisted of the President, Mrs. Lincoln, Mr. Welles, Mr. Stanton and two other gentlemen.

For some half-hour the demonstrations were of a physical character—tables were moved, and a picture of Henry Clay, which hangs on the wall, was swayed more than a foot, and two candelabra, presented by the Dey of Algiers to President Adams, was twice raised nearly to the ceiling. At length loud rappings was heard directly beneath the President's feet, and Mr. Shockle stated that an Indian desired to communicate. " I shall be happy to hear what his Indian majesty has to say, " replied the President, "for I have recently received a deputation of our red brethren, and it was the only delegation, black, white or blue, which did not volunteer some advice about the conduct of the war. " The medium then called for a pencil and paper, which were laid upon the table, and afterwards covered with a handkerchief. Presently knocks were heard, and the paper was uncovered. To the surprise of all present, it read as follows:

" Haste makes waste, but delays cause vexations. Give vitality by energy. Use every means to subdue. Proclamations are useless. Make a bold front, and fight the enemy; leave traitors at home to the care of loyal men. Less note of preparation, less parade and policy-talk, and more action.—HENRY KNOX. "

" That is not Indian talk, Mr. Shockle, " said the President. " Who is Henry Knox? "

The medium, speaking in a strange voice, replied, " The first Secretary of War. "

" Oh, yes; General Knox, said the President. Stanton, that message is for you; it is from your predecessor. I should like to ask General Knox to tell us when this rebellion will be put down."

The answer was oracularly indefinite. The spirit said that Napoleon thought one thing, Lafayette another, and that Franklin differed from both.

" Ah, " exclaimed the President, " opinions differ among the saints as well as among the sinners. Their talk is very much like the talk of my cabinet. I wish the spirits would tell us how to catch the Alabama? "

The lights almost instantaneously became so dim that it was impossible to distinguish the features of any one in the room, and on the large mirror over the mantlepiece, there appeared a sea-view, the Alabama, with all steam up; flying from the pursuit of another large steamer. Two merchantmen in the distance were seen partially destroyed by fire. The picture changed, and the Alabama was seen at anchor under the shadow of an English fort, from which an English flag was flying. The Alabama was floating idly, not a soul on board, and no signs of life visible about her. The picture vanished, and, in letters of purple, appeared, "The American people demand this of the English aristocracy."

"So England is to seize the Alabama, finally?" said the President. "It may be possible, but Mr. Welles, don't let one gunboat or one monitor less be built. Well, Mr. Shockle," continued he, "I have seen strange things, and heard rather odd remarks, but nothing that convinces me, except the pictures, that there is anything very heavenly about all this. I should like, if possible, to hear what Judge Douglas says about this war."

After an interval of about three minutes, Mr. Shockle rose quickly from his chair, and stood behind it. Resting his left arm on the back, his right into his bosom, he spoke in a voice such as no one could mistake who had ever heard Mr. Douglas. He urged the President to throw aside all advisers who hesitated about the policy to be pursued, and said that if victory were followed up by energetic action, all would be well.

"I believe that," said the President, "whether it comes from spirit or human. It need not a ghost from 'the bourne from which no traveler returns' to tell that."

The President's Aversion to Blood-shed.

A striking incident in Mr. Lincoln's official life is related by Judge Bromwell, of Denver, who visited the White House in March, 1865. Mr. Seward and several other gentlemen were also present, and the President gradually came to talk on decisions of life and death. All other matters submitted to him, he declared, were nothing in comparison to these, and he added: "I reckon there never was a man raised in the country on a farm, where

they are always butchering cattle and hogs and think nothing of it, that ever grew up with such an aversion to
bloodshed as I have; and yet I've had more questions of
life and death to settle in four years than all the men who
ever sat in this chair put together. But I've managed to
get along and do my duty, as I believe, and still save most
of them, and there's no man knows the distress of my
mind. But there have been some of them I couldn't save
—there are some cases where the law must be executed.
There was that man —, who was sentenced for piracy and
slave-trading on the high seas. That was a case where
there must be an example, and you don't know how they
followed and pressed to get him pardoned, or his sentence
commuted? but there was no use of talking. It had to be
done; I couldn't help him; and then there was that —,
who was caught spying and recruiting within Pope's lines
in Missouri. That was another case. They beseiged me
day and night, but I couldn't give way. We had come
to a point where something must be done that would put
a stop to such work. And then there was the case of
Beal on the lakes. That was a case where there had to
be an example. They tried me every way. They
wouldn't give up; but I had to stand firm on that, and I
even had to turn away his poor sister when she came and
begged for his life, and let him be executed, and he was
executed, and I can't get the distress out of my mind yet."
As the kindly man uttered these words the tears ran down
his cheeks, and the eyes of the men surrounding him
moistened in sympathy. There was a profound silence in
which they rose to depart. Three weeks after, the **Presi**-
dent was killed.

Two Hundred and Fifty Thousand Passes to Richmond.

A gentlemen called upon President Lincoln before the fall of Richmond and solicited a pass for that place. "I should be very happy to oblige you," said the President, "if my passes were respected; but the fact is, I have, within the past two years, given passes to two hundred and fifty thousand men to go to Richmond, and not one has got there yet."

Hon. Leonard Swett's Reminiscenses.

" I saw him," says Mr. Swett, " early one morning, when the President, alluding to the proposed Emancipation Proclamation, invited me to sit down, as he wished to confer with me on the subject. The conference lasted until the time came for the Cabinet Council, and during the whole time Lincoln did all the talking. He did not really want my advice; he wanted simply so go over the ground with me.

During the conference the President read a very able letter from Robert Dale Owen, urging reasons why the War could never be gone through successfully without the Emancipation Proclamation. As Lincoln read it he remarked, 'this is a very able paper,' at the same time stating that he had prepared a paper on the same subject but that Owen's was much the abler of the two.

The President then offered to read letters of another kind,—letters complaining of his Administration, piling upon him the most frightful abuse for being a do nothing in the Presidential Chair. The reading of letters of this class occupied an hour. He also read a letter from the Frenchman Gasparin, who advised him to do nothing that was revolutionary, and urging the claims of legitimacy. He argued that the South were revolutionists, and asked whether a proclamation freeing the slaves might not render the Northerners revolutionists themselves.

Lincoln then reviewed the three kinds of letters, and also gave his own views as to the probable results of freeing the negroes, his great fear being that they might, thus freed, become an element of weakness to their liberators.

Before the interview was ended, I, pondering upon what Mr. Lincoln had said about having written something upon the subject of emancipation, made a guess that he had in the drawer before him the proclamation ready written, and I asked the President to let me see what he had prepared on the subject. Lincoln asked me not to press the request, and I abstained from doing so, but three weeks afterward, when the proclamation had been issued, the President acknowledged to me that my guess had been a correct one, and that the document was, at the time of the interview, lying in the very spot I had mentioned.

As soon as Lincoln saw that the negro slave could become a soldier he saw that he had the material out of which the Rebellion could be crushed, and it is my belief that from this time forward Lincoln had a clear sight of the victory that stood at the end of the War.

Speaking of Lincoln's habits, the Hon. Leonard Swett says, that the martyr-President was used to work all his life, but never to its dissipations. With him morning meant 6 o'clock a. m., and, as a rule, he had finished breakfast and was at work at 7 o'clock. What tore his heart most of all during the War was an approval of the death penalty. He had a horror of blood, and although he knew that under certain circumstances he could not avoid signing the death-warrant for desertion, it always caused him infinite pain to do so.

One morning Mr. Swett found him sitting in the "east room" before a pile of papers. They sat together, chatted and told stories. It was a Thursday, and Friday was always the day upon which deserters were shot. Suddenly Lincoln arose and said abruptly, "Swett, go out of here; to-morrow is butcher's day, and I've got to go through these papers, not to see if they are regular, but if I can't find something by which I can let them off."

The Triplets Lincoln Named.

In South Starksboro, Addison county, Vt., says the Burlington *Free Press*, there are residing triplets, sons of Leonard Haskins, born May 24, 1864, and named by President Lincoln. They have in their possession a letter from the hand of the martyr-President, and the names given were Abraham Lincoln, Gideon Welles and Simon Cameron. They are the children of American parents (who are still living) of limited circumstances, have led a very retired life, are robust, intelligent, and moral, and have always been total abstainers from liquor and profanity. There is an almost perfect resemblance between two who are light complexioned, while the other is a striking contrast, having dark hair and eyes.

Lincoln and the Colored People at Richmond.

G. F. Shepley gives the following interesting reminiscence:

After Mr. Lincoln's interview with Judge Campbell the

President about to return to the Wabash, I took him and Admiral Porter in my carriage. An immense concourse of colored people thronged the streets, accompanied and followed the carriage, calling upon the President with the wildest exclamations of gratitude and delight. He was the Moses, the Messiah, to the slaves of the South. Hundreds of colored women tossed their hands high in the air and then bent down to the ground weeping for joy. Some shouted songs of deliverance, and sang the old plantation refrains, which had prophesied the coming of a deliverer from bondage. "God bless you, Father Abraham!" went up from a thousand throats. Those only who have seen the paroxysmal enthusiasm of a religious meeting of slaves can form an adequate conception of the way in which the tears, and smiles, and shouts of these emancipated people evinced the frenzy of their gratitude to their deliverer. He looked at it all attentively, with a face expressive only of a sort of pathetic wonder. Occasionally its sadness would alternate with one of his peculiar smiles, and he would remark on the great proportion of those whose color indicated a mixed lineage from the white master and the black slave; and that reminded him of some little story of his life in Kentucky, which he would smilingly tell; and then his face would relapse again into that sad expression which all will remember who saw him during the last few weeks of the Rebellion. Perhaps it was a presentiment of his impending fate.

I accompanied him to the ship, bade him farewell, and left him, to see his face no more. Not long after, the bullet of the assassin arrested the beatings of one of the kindest hearts that ever throbbed in human bosom.

Lincoln's First Convictions of War—His Great Sadness·

The Hon. Leonard Swett, in an address before the Union Veteran Club at Chicago, gives the following interesting reminiscence:

I remember well the first time that the belief that war was inevitable took hold of Lincoln's mind. Some time after the election Lincoln asked me to write a letter to Thurlow Weed to come to Springfield and consult with him, (Lincoln). Mr. Weed came, and he, the President-elect, and myself had a meeting, in which Lincoln for the first time acknowledged that he was in possession of facts that showed that the South meant war. These facts consisted of the steps which the disaffected States were taking to spirit away the arms belonging to the Government, and, taking them into consideration, Lincoln was forced to the belief that his Administration was to be one of blood. As he made this admission his countenance rather than his words demonstrated the sadness which it occasioned, and he wanted to know if there was not some way of avoiding the disaster. He felt as if he could not go forward to an era of war, and these days were to him a sort of forty days in the wilderness, passed under great stress of doubt and, perhaps to him, of temptations of weakness. Finally, however, he seemed quietly to put on the armor and prepare himself for the great responsibility and struggle before him.

A Reminiscence of Lincoln.

Says a correspondent of the Chicago *Tribune*: Early in December, 1860, I was called to Springfield on business. It had then been ascertained that Mr. Lincoln was certainly the President-elect. He had just taken Gov. Yates' room in the State-House. As I was entering the State-House about 9 o'clock a. m., I met Mr. Lincoln on the steps, and he invited me to his rooms. After remaining alone in conversation with him until about 10 o'clock, two gentlemen from Memphis, Tenn., were ushered in and introduced by the Rev. Dr. —, of Springfield. They had been deputed by the Cotton Exchange of Memphis to visit Mr. Lincoln and ascertain what his policy would be towards the Southern States.

After a very satisfactory conversation of perhaps an hour, and as they were on the point of leaving, a loud rap was heard at the door, to which Mr. Lincoln responded, "Come in." But no one entered. After a short pause another and louder rap was heard, and Mr. Lincoln arose and opened the door, when an old gentleman, about 65 years of age entered, whose hand Mr. Lincoln grasped very cordially. They were old-time acquaintances, and, after mutual inquiries about friends and families, the old gentleman put his hand in the pocket of his old-fashioned, blue, swallow-tailed coat and took therefrom a large, beautiful apple, and said; "Abraham, here is an apple that Mary plucked from your favorite tree in the southwest corner of the orchard; and she asked me to hand it to you with her best wishes for your success and prosperity. As I have no time to spare, as I must leave for home, for I have a long distance to go, I thought I would call and see you for a few minutes. We have known each other for many years. You will soon leave for Washington, and we may never meet again. You are the President-elect. I rejoiced when you were nominated, I voted for you, and rejoiced still more when you were elected. I fear you will have great trouble. You must allow me to give you a few words of advice, as I have often done before. Abraham, you know what it cost our forefathers to secure our independence and establish the Union. Ours is the best Government on the face of the earth, and it must be preserved. But we want no bloodshed! We want no war! You must be kind to our Southern brethren. They are hot-headed, but good-hearted. They think slavery is endangered by your election. Treat them kindly, and tell them that your Administration will do them no wrong; that you will be the President of the whole country, and every constitutional right preserved. If they persist in their threat to dissolve the Union, then I charge you by the memory of our fathers, by the blood and sacrifices of the Revolution, by everything we prize in all our history, by your duty to posterity and the world, use all the power under Heaven at your command to crush every seed of dissolution and wipe out every traitor to our country!"

The brief speech was delivered while the two were standing facing each other, and in a distinct but nervous voice which thrilled every one present and brought tears to every eye.

With mutual "God bless you," the old man departed for his Macon (I think) County home, and but few words were spoken before we all separated.

How Lincoln Won the Nomination for Congress.

Old-time politicians, says a correspondent, will readily recall the heated political campaign of 1843 in the neighboring State of Illinois. The chief interest of the campaign lay in the race for Congress in the Capital district, which was between Hardin—fiery, eloquent and impetuous Democrat; and Lincoln—plain, practical and ennobled Whig. The world knows the result. Lincoln was elected.

It is not so much with his election as with the manner in which he secured his nomination with which we have to deal. Before that ever-memorable spring Lincoln vacillated between the courts of Springfield, rated as a plain, honest, logical Whig, with no ambition higher, politically than to occupy some good home office. Late in the fall of 1842 his name began to be mentioned in connection with Congressional aspirations, which fact greatly annoyed the leaders of his political party, who had already selected as the Whig candidate, one Baker, afterward the gallant Colonel, who fell so bravely and died such an honorable death on the battlefield at Ball's Bluff, in 1862. Despite all efforts of his opponents within his party the name of the "gaunt rail-splitter" was hailed with acclaim by the masses, to whom he had endeared himself by his witicisms, honest tongue, and quaint philosophy when on the stump or mingling with them in their homes.

The convention, which met in early spring in the city of Springfield, was to be composed of the usual number of delegates. The contest for the nomination was spirited and exciting. A few weeks before the meeting of the convention the fact was found by the leaders that the advantage lay with Lincoln, and that, unless they pulled some very fine wires, nothing could save Baker. They attempted to play the game that has so often won, by "convincing" delegates under instructions for Lincoln to violate them and vote for Baker. They had apparently succeeded. "The plans of mice and men aft gang aglee;" so it was in this case. Two days before the convention Lincoln received an intimation of this, and late at night indited the following letter. The letter was addressed to Martin Morris, who resides at Petersburg, an intimate friend of his, and by him circulated among those who were instructed for him at the county convention. It had the desired effect. The convention met, the scheme of the conspirators miscarried, Lincoln was nominated, made a vigorous canvass, and was triumphantly elected, thus paving the way for his more extended and brilliant conquests. This letter, Lincoln has often told his friends, gave him ultimately the Chief Magistracy of the Nation. He has also said that had he been beaten before the convention he would have been forever obscured. The following is a verbatim copy of the epistle:

"APRIL 14, 1843.—FRIEND MORRIS: I have heard it intimated that Baker has been attempting to get you or Miles, or both of you, to violate the instructions of the meeting that appointed you, and to go for him. I have insisted, and still insist, that this cannot be true. Surely Baker would not do the like. As well might Hardin ask me to vote for him in the convention. Again, it is said there will be an attempt to get up instructions in your county requiring you to go for Baker. This is all wrong. Upon the same rule why might not I fly from the decision against me in Sangamon, and get up instruction to their delegates to go for me? There are at least 1,200 Whigs in the county that took no part, and yet I would as soon stick my head in the fire as to attempt it. Besides if any one should get the nomination by such extraordinary means, all harmony in the district would inevitably be lost. Honest Whigs, (and very nearly all of them are honest) would not quietly abide such enormities. I repeat, such an attempt on Baker's part cannot be true. Write me at Springfield how the matter is. Don't show or speak ot this letter. A. LINCOLN. "

Mr. Morris did show the letter, and Mr. Lincoln always thanked his stars that he did.

Lincoln's Partner Giving up His Old Relics.

The following is a copy of an autograph letter of Abranam Lincolns' which was received by Capt. H. A. Parker, President of the Englewood Soldiers' Memorial Association from W. H. Herndon, former law partner of President Lincoln:

SPRINGFIELD, Ill., Oct. 10, 1860.—*Dear William*: I cannot give you details, but it is entirely certain that Pennsylvania and Indiana have gone Republican very largely. Penn. 25,000 & Ia. 5 to 10,000. Ohio of course is safe. Yours as ever, A. LINCOLN.

Accompanying the above is a leaf from Mr. Lincolns' boy copy-book. The two relics are explained in full by a letter from Mr. Herndon to Capt. Parker, of which the following is a copy:

SPRINGFIELD, Ill., Nov. 9, 1881.—*Mr. Parker*—MY DEAR SIR: Inclosed is a genuine letter from Lincoln, addressed to myself, dated the 10th day of October, 1860, a few days before Mr. Lincolns' election to the Presidency. The history of the letter is as follows: I was in Petersburg on the day the letter is dated, and in the evening, say at 7 o'clock, I was speaking to a large audience in the court house urging Lincoln's election. I had spoken about thirty minutes, when a runner handed me the letter, and I opened it in dead silence, thinking possibly that bad news had come to me, possibly Lincoln's defeat. However, the dead silence was soon broken by the reading of the letter, first to myself and then aloud, as loud as I could, and then there went up such yells, huzzas, such noise, such banging and thumping as were never heard in that house of justice before. The joy of the crowd, the noise of the yells, etc., were more eloquent than I was, and I got off the stand and quit my jabber in presence of the general joy. When Lincoln wrote the letter he knew that he was elected to the Presidential Chair. He must have been grateful to the people, and happy. I can see his feelings in his hand-writing; he trembled a little, was full of emotion, joy and happiness.

I hate to part with this letter. It is the last one I have, and no money could get it. I willingly give it to you for the purposes it is given—namely: to the Soldiers' Memorial Association of Englewood, Ill., and its uses, etc., etc. To me there is a long history in the letter and its glorious recollections.

Again, I send you a leaf of Mr. Lincoln's boy copybook —a book in which Mr. Lincoln put down his arithmetical sums worked out.

I was collecting the facts of Mr. Lincoln's life in 1865-6 and went into Coles County, Illinois, to see his step-mother; found the motherly, good old lady, and took down her testimony, etc., as material of his life, etc. During her examination she let drop, in her conversation, the fact that Mr. Lincoln when a boy had two copybooks, in which he wrote down his sums worked out, and wrote out in his literary one what seemed strong, beautiful or good. We, the Lincoln family and myself, commenced the search and found the arithmetical book, but not the other; it is gone, and gone forever. I willingly send you a leaf of said copybook for the use and purposes above, and for no other. I say this of the letter and the leaf. I would not spare them under any other consideration. God bless the soldier and his friend!

To keep the pieces, get two glasses and put the letter between them; have it framed, and the letter thus framed and between two glasses will last for ages hung on the wall. To keep the leaf and letter, get two glasses, say 6x7 inches for the latter, and 10x12 for the leaf—clean and clear glass like perfect window glass—put the paper and the leaf between the two glasses, hang up in the hall, and it will last for ages, keep a watch-out that too much light does not exhaust the ink: dry it out or up, etc. Hurriedly your friend. W. H. HERNDON.

Capture of Booth, the Assassin.

Capt. Edward P. Doherty, who commanded the detachment that captured Booth and Arnold after the assassination of President Lincoln, has given a very full account of how the capture was effected. The story is told as follows: After Garrett had designated the direction of the barn, Capt. Doherty said to Sergt. Boston Corbett: 'Dismount your men, detail a few to watch the house, and bring the remainder here.' Capt. Doherty then surrounded the barn with his men, and going to the front door, placed a lighted candle, which he had held in his hand for some time, near the front entrance of the barn. Unlocking the door, Capt. Doherty called upon those in the barn to come out and surrender, but no answer was made to this and subsequent frequent and loud demands of a like

character.   Capt. Doherty then passed among his senti-
nels who surrounded the barn, when he was informed that
whispering and the moving of hay had been heard from
the inside.

Capt. Doherty then said: ' If you don't come out, I'll
set fire to the building and burn you out.'   As there was
no answer even to this, Capt. Doherty ordered Corp. Newgarten to pile some shavings and hay in the opening, and
set fire to it.   While he was piling it up a voice said to
the corporal: ' If you come back there I'll put a bullet
through you.'   Capt. Doherty, who was standing near
Newgarten, then quietly ordered him to desist, and determined to wait till daylight before making any further demonstrations.

At this time quite a long conversation took place between Capt. Doherty and J. Wilkes Booth.   The former,
after hearing the threat of the latter, called again for a
surrender, when Booth replied: ' Who do you take us for?'
Capt. Doherty responded: ' It don't make any difference
who I take you for, I am going to arrest you.'   Then
Booth said: ' Boys, fetch me a stretcher.   Another stain
in our glorious banner.'

Walking around the barn and returning near the door
Capt. Doherty heard a whispered conversation between
Booth and Harrold from the inside.   Booth then said
aloud: ' I am crippled and alone; give me a chance for my
life; draw your men up at twenty-five paces and I will
come out.'

Capt. Doherty replied: 'I didn't come here to fight,
but to capture you.   I have fifty men here and can do it.'

In the meantime Harrold had approached the door,
when Capt. Doherty said to him, 'Let me see your hands,'

when Harrold put both hands out through the door and Capt. Doherty, seizing them, handed Harrold over to the corporal at the door.

While this conversation was going on, and as Capt. Doherty was in the act of taking Harrold out of the front door, the barn had been fired in the rear. The flames burst suddenly forth. Booth, who had left his position in the barn to the right of the opening referred to above, near the candle, took a position in the centre of the barn facing the door, and, raising his carbine, pointed it in the direction of Harrold and Capt. Doherty, when Sergt. Corbett, who was stationed at one of the openings in the barn to the left of Booth, observing the movement, leveled a large-sized Colt's revolver at Booth and fired, intending to hit him in the arm for the purpose of disabling him, but the ball entered his neck, about one inch from the same point as Booth shot president Lincoln.

On hearing the shot, and being at the time ignorant of the movement or intention of Booth, Capt. Doherty supposed that he had shot himself rather than surrender, when the officers rushed into the barn, and by the light of the burning building saw Booth with the carbine between his legs, one of his crutches having dropped, and Booth in the act of falling forward, when Captain Doherty caught him with both arms around the body and carried him outside of the barn, and laid him down; but the heat becoming too intense, Capt. Doherty ordered him removed under the veranda of the Garrett mansion.

Soldiers were then dispatched in different directions for doctors, but only one, Dr. Urquart, could be found, he arriving about 6 A. M., and, after probing the wound, pronounced it fatal, the ball having ranged upward, cutting a vital part.

From the time that Booth was shot, 5 o'clock, to the time he expired, two hours later, he spoke but once, and that was to Capt. Doherty, shortly before 6 o'clock, when he said to him, 'Hands.' Capt. Doherty lifted up his hands, when Booth looked at them for an instant, and, shaking his head, exclaimed, 'Useless, useless.' A short time after this he became unconscious, and so remained until he expired.

Capt. Doherty, after wrapping the body of Booth in his saddle blanket, sewed the blanket together with his own hands, and, having placed the body on a cart which was obtained from an old negro residing about two miles distant, proceeded with the body and the prisoner, Harrold to Belle Plain, where the Ide was awaiting the return of the command, which arrived at 6 P. M., when the Ide proceeded to Washington, where the body of Booth and the prisoner, Harrold, were turned over to the officers of the United States iron-clad monitor Montauk, Capt. Doherty having received orders from the department commander so to do. This was at 3 o'clock on the morning of the 27th.

In reference to the different statements that Booth was never captured nor killed, and that he is alive to-day, Capt. Doherty says that it is the sheerest nonsense in the world, as, in the first place, Capt. Doherty knew J. Wilkes Booth personally, and was in his company at the National hotel in Washington about two months previous to the assassination. In the second place, at the post mortem examination, held on the 27 of April, Booth was fully indentified by Dr. May, his attending physician, who had performed an operation upon his neck, and by Mr. Dawson, proprietor of the National hotel, where he boarded during his residence in Washington, and also by other well-known citizens, to the full satisfaction of the government.

In the third place, after the body of Booth was buried in a cell in the penitentiary at the arsenel in Washington, the remains were delivered over to his relatives four years later, upon application to President Johnson, and they now rest in the family vault near Baltimore, Md., thus proving that the members of his own family recognize the fact that the body lying there is the last mortal remains of J. Wilkes Booth.

Wilkes Booth's Pursuer.

Joseph B. Stewart, a lawyer, was the man who leaped on the stage of Ford's theatre in Washington on the night of April 14, 1865, and followed John Wilkes Booth behind the scenes into the alley where the saddled horse was in waiting. Everybody else in the theatre was dazed at what had occurred, or was thoughtful only of the wounded man.

Mr. Stewart sat with his family next to the orchestra rail to the right of the middle aisle. To his right, in the proscenium box of the second tier was President Lincoln. Mr. Stewart heard the fatal shot, and, looking up, saw the President's head fall forward on his bosom. The stage was empty. The next instant Booth stepped on the balustrade of the box to leap down to the stage. As he stood poised with a dagger in his hand, Stewart, who had had a slight acquaintance with him, recognized him, and at a glance and took in the situation.

Booth's spur was caught in some of the drapery, and as he fell to the stage his back was toward the spectators. The words "*Sic semper Tyrannis*" were uttered before his feet touched the stage. He sprang up and brandishing the dagger, strode diagonally across the stage to the opposite side. As he arose Mr. Stewart sprang to the top of the orchestra rail, but his foot slipped. He lost an instant in mending his hold, and then leaped over the intervening space to the foot-lights. Had he known the position of the rear entrance to the theatre, he could have reached it as soon as Booth did. As it was, he was compelled to follow the fugitive diagonally to the left and then back across the stage behind the scenes.

The door was shut in his face, and he could not readily open it. When he did, he saw Booth springing into the saddle. The horse's head was toward a brick wall. Stewart sprang forward to grasp the left rein. As he did so Booth turned the animal toward the right, and, backing it as it turned, its rump threw Stewart against the wall. Then came a race across the court yard toward a sharp turn that led to the alley opening into F sreet. The horse could not be galloped in this yard, and Stewart nearly caught up with it on its left side, but was again crowded against a wall. He was between the horse and the wall.

Booth made one stroke at his pursurer with the dagger that he yet held, but seemed to be anxious to get away without shedding more blood.

While the latter was yet struggling for the bridle-rein, Booth arrived at the mouth of the alley, and, putting his horse into a gallop, soon rattled out of sight.

Subsequently Stewart was asked by a friend why he was so anxious to get hold of the bridle.

"Because," the giant said, "I knew exactly what to do if I got hold of the bit. I would have thrown the horse over on his back. Yet I think," he added, "it was very fortunate that I did not catch him. The theatre was filled with soldiers. The feeling after the first moment of inaction was one of intense bitterness. They came pouring over the stage and out of the stage door. If Booth had been there he would have been shot into pieces. Many of themselves would have accidentally fallen victims to their reckless fury. I suppose that if I had stood there holding him when they came out my virtues would now be proclaimed to a careless world on a piece of marble. Besides, it was better as it was. If Booth had been killed, then the plot for the assassination would never have been discovered."

Secretary Usher's Reminiscences of Lincoln—An Interesting Chapter.

Secretary Usher, who was a member of Lincolns' Cabinet, and an old friend, gives the following interesting reminiscences:

LINCOLN AS A LAWYER.

Lincoln belonged to the reasoning class of men. He dealt with his own mind and turned things over there, seeking the truth until he established it and it became a conviction. As a lawyer, he never claimed everything for his client. He stated something of both sides of the case. I have known him to say! "Now, I don't think my client is entitled to the whole of what he claims. In this point or that point he may have been in error. He must rebate something of his claim." He was also very careful about giving personal offense, and if he had something severe to say, he would turn to his opponent or to the person about to be referred to and say: " I don't like to use this language,' or, ' I am sorry that I have to be hard on that gentleman;' and, therefore, what he did say was thrice as effective, and very seldom wounded the person attacked. Throughout Mr. Lincoln's life that kind of wisdom attended him, and made him the great and skillful politician he was in handling people. He had a smooth, manly, pleasing voice, and when arguing in court, that voice attracted the jury, and did not tire them, so that they followed his argument throughout. He was not a graceful man. He would lean on the back of a chair, or put the chair behind him, or stand hipshotten, or with arms akimbo, but yet there was a pleasure in listening to him, because he seemed so unmercenary.

LINCOLN'S AMBITION.

I do not think Lincoln was ambitious at all. It seems to me that his object in life was no greater than to make a living for his family. The dream of avarice never crossed him. He took no initial steps to reach the Presidency or the Senate, and was rather pushed forward, than a volunteer. I can't recall in those days when he attended court that he ever spoke about himself or took any satisfaction in victory over an adversary, or repeated any good thing he had done or said. As a partisan he always reasoned for the good of the party, and not concerning his own advancement. Consequently, when the people had made up their minds that there was talent in him, of a remarkable kind, they came to his assistance with a spotaneity and vehemence that was electrical. He reaped the great reward of unselfishness as few men have ever done.

MR. LINCOLN'S NATURE.

I can recall a certain incident that illustrates Lincoln's nature. Somewhere near the town of Parris there was a Whig population, with strong prejudices in favor of protecting slavery. These people liked Lincoln, and believed in him, and saw with pain that he was becoming a Radical. They came to him during court and said: 'We want you to come up and talk to us. We don't want to quarrel with you, and will hear all you have to say; but something must be wrong when as fair a man as you is drifting over to Abolitionism.' 'Very well,' said Mr. Lincoln, 'I will come up on such a day and give you my views.' Lincoln went on that day, and made a temperate, sweet-toothed, cordial address on the issues of the day. He said: 'My friends, I perceive you will not agree with me, but that ought to make no difference in our relations with each other. You hear me, as you always have, with kindness, and I shall respect your views, as I hope you will mine.' They heard Lincoln through, and dismissed him with respect, but did not agree with him. There was another person up there by the name of Stephens, who was lame, and he undertook to emphasize Lincoln's views, and put his foot in it. A certain doctor, of Southern origin, interrupted Stephens, and said he would thrash him. Stevens turned around and replied, 'Well, doctor, you can thrash me, or do anything of a violent sort to me, if you don't give any of your pills.' Lincoln used to tell this story with a good deal of delight. You see, in those days the settlers in Illinois would live in the edges of the timber, which grew in spots and patches, and left naked prairie between the groves. It was at such a place that Lincoln made that speech on the slavery question.

LINCOLN AND THE LADIES.

He was almost wholly possessed with a sense of duty and responsibility. He was not shy in the company of ladies, but I don't think he thought anything about them until they came before him as guests and callers. Some of the women gave him a good deal of trouble. Some of his wife's people were southerners, and public attacks were made on them; as, for instance, it was said that one of them had gone through the lines with a pass from Mr. Lincoln, and taken a quantity of medicine, etc. I remember that an old partner in law of mine brought his wife to Washington, and they wanted to see Mr. Lincoln. There was a great crowd awaiting around his door, but the doorkeeper admitted us at once, and Mr. Lincoln came forward with both hands extended and shook the lady's hand, rather divining that she was the wife of my partner. He told a little anecdote or two, and said some quaint things, and when the lady came out she said to me: "Why I don't think that he is an ugly man at all." He was almost a father to his wife. He seemed to be possessed of the notion that she was under his protection, and that he must look out for her like a willful child.

LINCOLN'S TEMPER.

I remember one event showing Lincoln's temper. He had issued a proclamation stating that when one-tenth of the voters of a Congressional district, or a part of a State, resumed their position in the Union, and elected a member of Congress, they should be recognized as much as the whole constituency. Chase remarked. 'Instead of saying voters, I suggest that you put in citizens!' I saw in a minute what Chase was driving at. This question had arisen as to who were citizens, and Mr. Bates, the Attorney-General, had pronounced negroes to be citizens. The law of the administration, therefore, was, that negroes were included in citizenship. As I walked away from the Cabinet that day Chase was at my side, and he said: Mr Usher, we must stick to it that citizens, and not voters, be named in that proclamation.' I turned about when we had got to the Treasury, and walked back on the plank which at that time led to the White House, and I told Lincoln that Chase was very pertinacious about the word citizens instead of voters. 'Yes' said Lincoln, 'Chase thinks that the negroes, as citizens, will all vote to make him President.'

LINCOLN'S SADNESS.

Lincoln was, in his fixed quality, a man of sadness. If he were looking out of a window when alone, and you happened to be passing by and caught his eye, you would generally see in it an expression of distress.

He was one of the greatest men who ever lived. It has now been many years since I was in his Cabinet, and some of the things that happened there have been forgotten, and the whole of it is rather dreamy. But Lincoln's extraordinary personality is still one of the most distinct things in my memory. He was as wise as a serpent. He had the skill of the greatest statesman in the world. Everything he handled came to success. Nobody took up his work and brought it to the same perfection.

HIS KINDNESS.

Lincoln had more patience than anybody around him.

Sometimes, when we were considering a thing of importance in the Cabinet, his little son would push open the door and come in with a drum and beat it up and down the room, giving us all a certain amount of misery. Mr. Lincoln, however, never ordered the boy to be taken out, but would say: 'My son, don't you think you can make a little less noise?' That Thaddeus was a stubborn little chap. We could not make up with him when he got offended. Robert was as well-behaved a young man as I have ever seen. He went to Hartford and graduated, and we entertained high respect for him.

SEWARD AND LINCOLN.

I think that Lincoln had a real fondness and admiration for Seward. There was no suspicion or rivalry whatever, between them. Seward supported Lincoln in every position or scruple that he had. My impression is, that those two men were as cordial and intimate as any two persons of such prominence could be.

After Caleb Smith, of Indiana, was made a member of the Cabinet, he desired me to be his Assistant Secretary. Mr. Smith was nominated District Judge of the United States in the course of time, and then Mr. Lincoln promoted me at Smith's request. I was in the Cabinet somewhat more than two years, and a part of the time was under Mr. Johnson. That Cabinet was very ill-assorted. My predecessor, Judge Smith, was a kind man, but without much discrimination as to his followers. There hardly was ever such a thing as a regular Cabinet meeting in the sense of form. Under Johnson and under Grant, I have seen a table with chairs placed in regular order around it, as if for Cabinet council. Nothing of that kind ever occurred in Mr. Lincolns' Cabinet. Seward would come in and lie down on a settee. Stanton hardly ever stayed more than five or ten minutes. Sometime Seward would tell the President the outline of some paper he was writing on a State matter. Lincoln generally stood up and walked about. In fact, every member of that Cabinet ran his own Department in his own way. I don't suppose that such a historic period was ever so simply operated from the center of powers. Lincoln trusted all his subordinates and they worked out their own performances. "I regard Seward," said Mr. Usher, "as on the whole the strong man of the Cabinet, the counsel of the President."

LINCOLN AND MRS. FREMONT.

Well, there was the case of John C. Fremont. He had made up his mind to run a little enterprise of his own. When he got into Missouri he soon quarreled with Frank Blair, and Montgomery Blair started on to St. Louis. Meantime Mrs. Fremont came East, passing Blair on the road, and the same night she arrived went up to the President. She demanded to know what Montgomery Blair had gone to Missouri for. Mr. Lincoln said he didn't know. 'Has he gone out to remove my husband?' said Mrs. Fremont. 'You cannot remove Gen. Fremont. He would not be removed.' Mr. Lincoln instantly began to talk about the difficulties of making a journey from St. Louis City to Washington alone. Three or four times during the conversation she repeated, 'Gen. Fremont can not be removed.' Lincoln evaded that part of the talk every time, and she left unsatisfied.

HOW LINCOLN BECAME PRESIDENT.

Mr. Lincoln became President mainly on the score of his debate with Douglas. He had never been in any great prominence as an office-holder.   His thorough-going devotion to his party brought him universal good-will, however, and he grew so harmoniously into the advocacy of Republican principles and opposition to Douglas' notion of squatter sovereignty, that there was a general desire to see him come forward and debate with Douglas.   I can tell you something interesting about the debate.   Lincoln had no money.   He was in no position to match a man of Douglas' financial resources.   The people in Lincoln's following, however, put their hands in their pockets and subscribed for a band of music to appear with him, and that band was procured in Indiana.   They put the band on a wagon to send it by the roads from point to point of meeting.   Douglas meantime came on to New York and borrowed $100,000.   I think he got some of it from Ben Wood and Fernando Wood.   He then took a special train of cars and made a sort of triumphal tour of the State, designing to carry the Senatorship by storm.   Lincoln said after the contest was over with a certain serious grimness, 'I reckon that the campaign has cost me fully $250.' It was generally understood in the west that the same campaign cost Douglas $100,000.   Lincoln's speeches against Douglas were extemporaneous, and he never revised them.   My impression is that young McCullagh, now an editor in St. Louis, was the stenographer of Lincoln's speeches.   Douglas did revise his remarks.   They met seven times, if I remember.   Lincoln reasoned so closely and carefully on Douglas' false statements that he came out of the campaign covered with respect, and instantly the movement started to make him President. 'I think it is due," said Mr. Usher, "to Mr. Seward's memory to say that his extreme views on the slavery question help-d to beat him."

CARELESS OF HIS LIFE.

Lincoln was too careless. He would go out of his house at night and walk over to the War Department, where Stanton was receiving dispatches unattended. I said to him: "Lincoln, you have no business to expose yourself in this way. It is known that you go out at midnight and return here sometimes at two o'clock in the morning from the War Department. It would be very easy to kill you." The President replied that if anybody desired to assassinate him he did not suppose any amount of care would save him.

LINCOLN'S PLAN OF RECONSTRUCTION.

"Lincoln would have made," says Mr. Usher, "a powerful white Republican party in every Southern State. He had that in him which would have made the Southern people support him in preference to the radical Northern politicians. Lincoln would have said in private to their leaders, 'You will have to stand in with me and help me out; otherwise Sumner and Stevens and those fellows will beat us both.' He would have said, 'You go back home and start some schools yourselves for the negroes, and put them on the route to citizenship. Let it be your own work. Make some arrangements to give them some land ultimately out of the public domain in your States. In that way you will have them your friends politically, and your prosperity will not be embarrassed.' Only Mr. Lincoln could have carried out this platform. His temperament, eminence and quality all adapted him for such a great part.

Abraham Lincoln as a Lover.

A writer to the Springfield *Republican* gives the following exceedingly interesting account of the early loves of Abraham Lincoln:

The death of Mrs. Lincoln at the home of that sister where she was first met and was courted by her future husband, closes the family life of the great President. She was not his first or his deepest love. That distinction belongs to Ann Rutledge, whose father was the founder of New Salem, on the Sangamon, a village which is now deserted. Rutledge was one of the famous South Carolina families, and his daughter, four years younger than Lincoln, seems to have impressed the whole community as a lovely and refined girl, unaffected, "a blonde in complexion, with golden hair, cherry-red lips, and a bonny blue eye," says McNamara. McNamara was the lover who first won her heart. He went home to New York to take west his parents, but was detained some years in New York. In the mean time Lincoln pressed his suit, and the girl's parents doubted whether McNamara would ever come back; she gave her love to Lincoln, but insisted on waiting for a formal release from McNamara before marriage. This waiting told upon her sensitive organism, her health declined, and she died of what was called brain fever on Aug. 25, 1835. This was the great grief of Lincoln's youth. His reason was unsettled and his friend, Bowlin Greene, had to take him off to a lonely log cabin and keep him until he recovered his sanity. Then was when he learned the poem beginning:

Oh, why should the spirit of mortal be proud?

An old friend who asked him after his election to the

Presidency if it was true that he loved and courted Ann Rutledge, got this reply:

"It is true—true; indeed I did. I have loved the name of Rutledge to this day. It was my first. I loved the woman dearly. She was a handsome girl; would have made a good, loving wife; was natural and quite intellectual, though not highly educated. I did honestly and truly love the girl, and think often, often of her now."

McNamara returned soon after her death, lived near the little burying ground, and in 1866 pointed out the grave of Ann Rutledge to Mr. Herndon. This affair had a marked effect upon Lincoln's life, and added to its somber tone; but it probably had also a deeper meaning in purifying and ennobling his inner nature.

Mr. Lincoln, who by this time was a member of the legislature, and about 27, next "paid attentions" to a Miss Owens, a smart young woman of some avoirdupois, who once told him that she thought he was "lacking in the smaller attentions, those little links which make up the great chain of woman's happiness," because he dangled along by her side once when they were going up a hill, and allowed her friend, Mrs. Bowlin Greene, to "carry a big, fat child, and crossly disposed," up the hill. A still more untoward incident happened once at Mrs. Able's, a sister of Miss Owens. Lincoln had sent word to Able's that he was coming down to see Miss Owens. She, girl fashion, to test her lover, went off "to Graham's," about a mile and a half. When Lincoln came and was so informed, he asked if Miss Owens did not know he was coming. Mrs. Able said no, but one of her *enfantes terribles* promptly replied: "Yes, ma, she did, for I heard Sam tell her so."

"Lincoln sat awhile and then went about his business,"

says Lamon's account.   Letters exist from Lincoln to Miss Owens in 1836 and 1839, in one of which he says:

" If you feel yourself in any degree bound to me, I am now willing to release you, provided you wish it; while, on the other hand, I am willing and even anxious to bind you faster, if I can be convinced that it will, in any considerable degree, add to your happiness.   This, indeed, is the whole question with me.   Nothing would make me more miserable than to believe you miserable—nothing more happy than to know you were so."

This is the language of an honorable man, a cool lover, and a practiced hand in the English language.   Miss Owens declined his hand and lived to marry another man at her home in Kentucky, and have two sons in the rebel army.   Lamon prints also a letter of Lincoln to Mrs. O. H. Browning, in 1838, reviewing this affair in terms, it must be confessed, brutally derogatory to the young woman's personal appearance and parts.   Lamon speaks of its defective spelling, but there are only one or two misspelled words in it, and these, likely enough, by accident.   Lincoln was evidently mortified by his rejection and ignobly attempted to represent to Mrs. Browning (the wife of his new-found legislative friend), that the object of his affections had been unworthy of them.

It was not two years (1839) before another Springfield matron, Mrs. Ninian W. Edwards, had a Kentucky sister to live with her, Mary Todd, daughter of Robert S. Todd, of Lexington.   Miss Todd was of distinguished family in both States, her mother had died young, and she had been educated by " a French lady."   She had a keen sense of the ridiculous, was sharp, ambitious, high-tempered: according to Lamon, " high-bred, proud, brilliant, witty, and with a will that bent everyone else to her purposes, she took Lincoln captive the very moment she considered it expedient to do so. She was ambitious to be the wife of a president, and was courted by Douglas till she dismissed him for his bad morals. She said of one of her mates who had married a wealthy old gentleman, " I would rather marry a good man, a man of mind, with hope and bright prospects ahead for position, fame and power, than to marry all the horses, gold and bones in the world." Lincoln and Miss Todd became engaged, though a pretty sister of Edwards, came near shipwrecking even this match. Pretty girls must have been distressingly thick in those days, when Kentucky was sending her best blood into Illinois. Lincoln felt the Edwards attachment so strongly that he begged to be released by Miss Todd (the Edwards girl married another man, for Lincoln never mentioned it to her), and he "ran off the track" again, to use the expression by which he once described his attack of insanity. He was " crazy as a loon " for nearly a year, and did not attend the session of the legislature of 1841-42, to which he had been chosen. They had to keep knives and razors away from him. As he came out of it, the Edwardses advised Abe and Mary not to marry, as they were unfitted to each other, and probably in consequence of this advice they—went and married on " one or two hours' notice." Lincoln told his friend Matheny, who made out the license, "Jim, I shall have to marry that girl," and he " looked as if he was going to the slaughter," and said he was " driven into it " by the Edwards family. But, perhaps, these expressions ought not to be taken too seriously. Lamon prints letters from Lincoln to **Speed** earlier in the year, indicating his embarrassing position, his "great agony," as Lamon calls it.

The "Shields Duel" was fought a month or two before the marriage, and was occasioned by Miss Todd's satirical sketches in *The Sangamon Journal*. These sketches were dated from the "Lost Township," a humorous expression of indefiniteness in locality which had a local point, and were written in vernacular and signed " Rebecca." The last one was in verse and signed "Cathleon." That Miss Todd was no green western girl is evinced by the spirit of these sketches of local life, which are reproduced in " Lamons Life of Lincoln. " She teased Shields in them, and he demanded to know the author. Lincoln accepted the responsibility.

Reminiscences of Lincoln and Stanton.

A correspondent of the *Philadelphia Press* gives the following interesting reminiscences of the great War President, and the "Watch Dog " of the War Office:

The Cabinet in which Mr. Stanton found himself, after Senator Cameron's voluntary retirement, (and Secretary Cameron fully possessed and always retained the confidence of Mr. Lincoln,) was a conglomeration of able men, several of whom had been themselves candidates for the Presidency, notably Chase, Seward and Bates. And when Mr. Lincoln was indulging what he called the "drifting policy," he would not, for months at a time, call any meeting of his Cabinet. And yet Lincoln is the man of whom Charles Francis Adams wrote, that Mr. Lincoln got the credit for all the statesmanship furnished by William H. Seward! Mr. Seward, in one of his pilgrimages to Auburn, where he was wont to retire semi-occasionally, as

Conkling goes to Utica when he has any special utterances intended for the public ear; on one of these historical occasions, after speaking in his " mediæval way " of what a " singularly pure young man " Gideon Welles must be, the optimistic Secretary of State delivered himself of a brilliant eulogy on Edwin M. Stanton, in which he spoke of him as the " Divine Stanton." The great War Minister deserved all the encomiums lavished on him then and at a later period during the War, by the gifted son of New York. To my mind the pre-eminently strong men of that period were Lincoln, Stanton, and Stevens. Stanton came into office under an extraordinary condition of politics. The old public functionary, J. Buchanan, who sat at Washington, "like an old bread-and-milk poultice, and drew the Rebellion to a head," had reluctantly consented to redeem the latest hours of his administration by taking into his counsels Dix and Stanton. At this the North breathed more freely, for it was a guarantee that there would be no open or actual surrender of the Government itself to the Davises, the Toombses, the Jake Thompsons, and the fire-eating crew generally and particularly.

Mr. Stanton had resumed the practice of the law after Mr. Lincoln's inauguration in the City of Washington, and had little expectation of being called into a Republican Cabinet. He felt stung at the audacity with which the Democracy had turned the sharp corner, and at once became the apologists, advocates and servants of an aristocracy built upon the back of the African slave.

His words were few in accepting the trust offered him by Mr. Lincoln, but they were to the purpose, and from that hour these two wonderful men, Lincoln and Stanton, were as close together as if they had been born " Siamese

twins." Lincoln's greatness very readily detected the virtues—the solid gold—in what he called "affirmative men."

Secretary Stanton was the earliest at his desk in the
morning and the latest to leave it. Many a night Mr.
Lincoln would slip out of the front door of the White
House and go alone over to the War Office, and these two,
absorbed in the conduct of the War, would listen to click
of the telegraph and read dispatches till daybreak. They
were completely *en rapport*, as the following incident will
demonstrate: Rev. Mr. X. had a soft billet as chaplain in
one of the Philadelphia hospitals. He had a sick wife.
Stanton had ordered the Rev. Mr. X. to be sent to the Dry
Tortugas, or some equally disagreeable place in Florida,
in the month of June. He came to me in great distress—
the preacher. He said: "You must go with me to Mr.
Lincoln. He is a kind-hearted man. He will surely not
send me away under the circumstances, with my wife
unable to make a Southern journey in summer." I went.
The Rev. Mr. X. went too. The White House was not
difficult of access, and I laid the matter before the good
old man with as much aplomb as possible. Mr. Lincoln
paused a moment and said: "Rev. Mr. X., this seems
like a hard case. I will see what I can do." He then
wrote in his plain, homely way on a blank card:

SECRETARY STANTON: See and hear Mr. L. in the matter of the
Rev. Mr. X. If the exigencies of the service permit, keep the Rev.
Mr. X. where he is now.   A. LINCOLN.

The great War Minister had just entered his office as
we ascended the steps of the old office in the War Department—gone now, covered over with the wing of modern
improvement—armed with the President's note, which

we regarded as a complete extinguisher or "squelcher" on the irrascible Stanton.

The Rev. X. expected a storm, nor was he mistaken. Stanton stood straight as an arrow, a cross, apparently, between John Knox, Thomas Carlyle and Martin Luther. He glared at the Rev. X., who had the reputation of always wanting "soft snaps." He only mollified his manner slightly toward us; extending his hand, he curtly said: "Well, what now?"

I handed him the card, with Mr. Lincoln's request in writing. His eyes flashed fire, and he dashed out in his jerky utterances these words:

"I won't do it, and you can tell him so." He tore the card up, and thew its fragments into the basket and continued: "Go ' l Mr. Lincoln I know what the exigencies of the service require, and the Rev. Mr. X. shall go where I order him to go."

The Rev. X. looked stunned, stupefied and distracted. I got him by the coat-sleeve and said: "Come, we will see about this."

I was hot. Had not the President of the United States been treated with contempt by his own cabinet officer? Fast as we could go there we hurried back, breathless to Mr. Lincoln and said:

"Why, Mr. President, Stanton is a hog. He tore up your order. Can you stand this?"

"Well," the kind old patriot replied with a twinkle in his eye. "I reckon I can. I never did have much influence with this administration!"

We retired in good order, and the Rev. Mr. X. resigned his office as chaplain the next day, and doubtless can be found preaching the Gospel somewhere now in "the pines"

of West Jersey. The next time I saw Secretary Stanton
he called me to him, and said:

"Young man, you may have thought me unreasonable
in that preacher's case, but I always have a good reason
for my actions."

Stanton was in temperament what the phrenologists call
"nervous sanguine, strongly marked lymphatic. He was
short in stature, with the general evidence of the English
bull dog in his make up." But he had a heart in him as
big as an ox. He would travel a thousand miles to undo
an injury if he felt sure he had acted unjustly toward a
human being. He knew what war was and he never used
ottar of roses. He had no patience with that officer who
would sign a voucher on honor (as they do in the army)
for a dollar more than he had honestly expended, and he
was like the wrath of God, slow but sure, on the trail of
that man caught robbing his Government in the hour of
the country's direst need. "How do you like Senator
——" I asked, naming a rich man with the Senatorial
purple around his neck, albeit it had cost him a pile of
money to get the "purple."

"Like him!" thundered the watch dog of the War
Office. "Like him! Why I had two of his pals in the
Old Capital Prison for selling the same vessel load of oats
three times to the same quartermaster, and if Lincoln had
not been so kind-hearted I would have had Senator ——
in the Old Capital Jail, too." But he could be just, even
in his wrath. John P. Hale, the most humorous and
gifted story-teller I ever knew, took $8,000 for getting a
Rebel out of Old Capital Prison. Some interested parties, possibly hoping to get the money back, began proceedings, intending at least, to disgrace Hale, then Senator

from New Hampshire. The whole matter was left to Secretary Stanton. He took a whole day to hear the evidence and his decision was prompt, and in these words:

" Senator Hale was offered $8,000 for his legal services. He earned it as a lawyer. That is all there is in this case."

The Secretary was very friendly with John W. Forney, and held him in high esteem, for Mr. Forney's early and constant fidelity to Lincoln's Administration in his two papers—" both daily! " Dan Dougherty was also a great favorite with the War Minister. If Mr. Lincoln had lived John W. Forney would not have abandoned Republicanism. The love of Stanton and Lincoln for each other was steadfast and unquestioning. They were two minds with but a single thought—and that was to crush out the rebellion.

With Stanton the lightning came first, the thunder afterward. He did not hesitate to put detectives into the White House to watch Andy Johnson, at which the tailor of Tennessee has been known to " cuss " a blue streak. It was at the suggestion of Senator Sumner and other Senators, notably Zach Chandler, that he barricaded the War Office and refused entrance to Gen. Lorenzo Thomas *ad interim* appointment of Johnson. It was General Lorenzo Thomas, who was told by a citizen of Delaware "that the eyes of Delaware were on him," and Lorenzo belittled the occasion, great and historic as it was, by swearing that he, Gen. Thomas and Secretary Stanton, had taken a drink of whisky together when " Lorenzo the Brave " demanded the office. This " soft impeachment " was never denied by the Secretary. It was while " holding the fort " in the War Office that Charles Sumner sent to Stanton the well-remembered telegram—viz:

SENATE CHAMBER—*Hon. Edwin M. Stanton, Secretary of War:*
Stick——   CHARLES SUMNER.

And he stuck. The pressure of these terrible times told on Stanton's iron constitution. It would necessarily tell on anybody not made in all parts of Bessemer Steel. Stanton thought Grant at first sided with Andy Johnson, and a question of veracity arose between them. It was hard for Stanton to forgive, and he never forgave Grant, unless it was when Grant sent him the ermine of the Supreme Court on his deathbed. But Grant was a proud man—so was Stanton, and their differances could have been reconciled had either been inclined to yield. While sitting in his sanctum at the War Office during the eventful summer of the "blockade" at the War Department, I suggested that Republics were ungrateful. He replied with sadness, that he never expected to be understood while he lived; that the populace had not changed greatly in the centuries since it cried "Hosanna" one day and "Crucify Him," the next. He seemed to feel sure of his place in history, but ever spoke of the politicians with fine scorn. He never seemed to me to be the same man after the death of Lincoln. An Administration guided by the hand of a great soldier, rather than a great statesman, had few charms for a trained intellect like Stanton's—the soldier element pressed to the fore and the civilian's place seemed to be in the rear. He never murmured, unless it was when he said: "Great deeds are not soon forgotten, but those who do them may be forgotten any hour."

Edwin M. Stanton gloried in his lack of riches. Millions had touched his palms, and massive fortunes adhered to the hands of those who surrounded him. He once quoted what seemed to be a sublime saying of Aristotle, to the effect that only those " who were rich because they could not help it, need be ashamed of it; but those who of their own choice had remained poor had a right to glory in it. "

These are the last words I ever heard the great-hearted Stanton utter. He was offered a retainer of $10,000 for an argument in one phase of the celebrated Credit Mobilier case; but he was either too feeble physically to prepare the case, or he distrusted the integrity of the cause he was asked to argue, and declined the fee. When it was found that Stantan had left no fortune save a stainless name to his children, Senator Chandler, of Michigan, soon repaired the broken fortunes of the great War Minister by making his family independent. It was only three days before he died that Gen. Grant, President of the United States, placed upon the broad shoulders of Edwin M. Stanton the ermine of the Supreme Court. But even this tardy justice came too late, but it may have softened the pangs of that great heart. Within forty-eight hours the soul of Judge Stanton had gone beyond the stars to the land where it is ever morning. It took America 280 years to build a memorial window to Sir Walter Raleigh, but not so long as 280 years will it take a grateful Republic, when she erects her Walhalla of her noble dead, to build a temple to commemorate Edwin M. Stanton's sublime devotion to duty. When future generations rise up to bless the great deeds of our heroes, and to keep green the memories of our bravest and best who fought for the liberation of humanity, there will be no name more reverently or tenderly cherished than the name of Edwin M. Stanton, the Christian, the hero, and the statesman, unless it be that name of that best of men, slain by Booth's bullet, with the prayer upon his lips "*that all men everywhere might be free.*"

INDEX

Page numbers in italics indicate illustrations.

Adams, Charles Francis, 238
Albany, New York, 168
Alley, John B., 151
Andersonville, Georgia, 109
Antietam, battle of, 130, 147
Appomattox, surrender at, 184
Army of the Potomac, 131,
    135–36
Arnold, Samuel, 219

Baltimore, Maryland, 113, 223
Bateman, Newton, 79, 80, 82
Bates, Edward, 66, 238
Beecher, Henry Ward, 159, 160
Bible, 19
Black Hawk War, 38–40, 41, 52
Blair, Francis ("Frank"), 155,
    231
Blair, Montgomery, 141–42, 231
Booth, John Wilkes, 246
    assassinates Lincoln, 186–87
    captured and killed, 219–23
    pursued by Joseph B.
      Stewart, 223–25
Boston Board of Trade, 140
Browning, O. H., Lincoln's
    letter to, 236
Buchanan, James, 239
Bull Run, second battle of, 120,
    147
Burnside, Ambrose, 105, 136

Cameron, Simon, 63, 210, 238
Campbell, John A., 155, 192
Campbell, Thompson, 60–61
Carlyle, Thomas, 241
Carpenter, F. B., 97–99, 105,
    130, 131, 153

Chandler, Zach, 243, 245
Charleston, South Carolina, 29
Chase, Salmon, 58, 114–15, 130,
    201, 203–4, 229, 238
Chelsea, Massachusetts, 85
Chicago Convention of 1860,
    70, 153, 167, 180
Chickamauga, battle of, 145
Cincinnati, Ohio, 113, 198
Clark, A. W., 109
Clary's Grove Boys, 48–49, 72,
    163
Cloud, Newton, 42
Cluse, George, 28–29
Coles County, Illinois, 74, 218
Colfax, Schuyler, 109, 182–83
Cooper Institute, 159
Corbett, Boston, 219, 221
Corwin, Thomas, 199–202
Credit Mobilier case, 245
Curtin, Andrew, 114–15
Cushing's Manual, 201

Davis, Jefferson, 154–55, 239
Dement, John, 42
Dickinson, Anna, 196
Dictionary of Congress, 179
Doherty, Edward P., 219–22
Dougherty, Dan, 243
Douglas, Stephen A., 42, 52, 81,
    178, 181, 198, 231–32
    monument to, *138*
Dubois, Jesse K., 42

Edwards, Ninian (Todd), 236
Elizabethtown, Kentucky, *16*
Emancipation Proclamation,
    97, 109–10, 130–31,
    146–47, 208

Englewood Soldiers' Memorial
    Association, 217
Essex County, New York, 129
Evansville, Indiana, 14, *158*,
    194

Fables (Aesop), 19
Field, Henry M., 159
Ford's Theatre, 184
Forney, John W., 243
Fort Donelson, 193
Fredericksburg, 135, 150–51
Fremont, John C., 231
Fremont, Mrs. John C., 231

Galena, Illinois, 30
Garfield, James, 58
Gasparin, Agenor-Etienne de,
    208–9
Gentryville, Indiana, *158*
Gettysburg, battle of, 147
Grant, Ulysses S., 94, 147, 149,
    150, 153, 230, 244, 245
Greene, William G., 25, 51,
    163–64

Hale, John P., 242–43
Halleck, Henry, 148
Hardin, John J., 42, 71, 215
Harlan, Justin, 46
Harper's Ferry, 109
Harrold, David, 220–21, 222
Haskins, Leonard, 210
Hazel, Caleb, 51
Herndon, William, 76, 217–19,
    235
Hilton Head, North Carolina,
    115
History of the Civil War
    (Abbott), 69
Hodgenville, Kentucky, *16*
Hogan, John, 42
Hooker, Joseph, Lincoln's letter
    to, 135–36
Hunter, R. M. T., 155–56, 192

Illinois Legislature, 40, 41–42,
    179

Jackson, Andrew, 32
Jefferson's Manual, 201
Johnson, Andrew, 153, 223, 230,
    243, 244

Kirkham's Grammar, 49
Knox, Henry, 205
Knox, John, 241

LaRue County, Kentucky, *16*
Lexington, Kentucky, 44
Life of Franklin, 19
Life of Henry Clay, 19–20
Life of Lincoln (Lamon), 236,
    238
Life of Washington (Ramsay),
    19
Life of Washington (Weems),
    14, 17, 20
Lincoln, Abraham
    Ann Rutledge and, 234–35
    assassination of, 132,
        147–48, 182, 184–88
    attends séance, 204–6
    autobiographical sketch by,
        179
    birthplace, *16*
    in the Black Hawk War,
        38–40, 52, 179
    books and, 14, 17, 19–20,
        41–42, 49
    children of, 105–8, 118,
        160–61, 230
    considers Emancipation
        Proclamation "central
        act," 131
    courtship and marriage,
        44–45, 236–38
    daily habits of, 209–10
    dream before assassination,
        147–48
    duel with James Shields,
        61–63, 71–72, 238

early jobs, 13–14, 22–24,
   27–29, 34, 37–38
early life, 13–52, 194–96
first political speech, 40
home in Springfield, *171*
as "Honest Abe," 31
honesty of, 14, 17, 22–23, 31,
   32–33, 52, 67, 68, 74, 82
in the Illinois Legislature,
   40–43, 179
inauguration as president,
   196
kindness of, 18–19, 26–27,
   229–30
as lawyer, 55–59, 64–65, 67,
   68–69, 72–74, 75–77, 82,
   179–80, 225–26
letter to Joseph Hooker,
   135–36
log cabin, 17, *36, 158*
memory of, 92–93
names Haskins triplets, 210
nomination for Congress,
   214–17
nomination for president,
   70, 153–54, 180
opinion of Grant, 94, 153
pardons soldiers, 134–35,
   150–51, 191, 210
plan for Reconstruction, 233
as postmaster, 20, 32–33, 179
professional life, 55–82
rejects Stanton's resignation,
   152
relationship with William
   Seward, 230–31
relieves William Rosecrans,
   145–46
religion and, 51, 80–82,
   85–86, *96,* 105, 107–8,
   118–21, 122, 139, 140,
   166–67
River Queen conference,
   155–56, 192
sadness of, 229

sense of humor, 39–40, 43,
   49, 111, 178, 179–80,
   197–98, 203–4
slaves' view of, 115–16,
   210–11
speech at Cooper Institute,
   159
speech to New Jersey
   Senate, 20
as storyteller, 77–79, 85–86,
   88–90, 91–92, 111–13,
   121–22
view of slave trade, 151–52
visits wounded soldiers,
   132–34
Lincoln, Mary (Todd), 44–45,
   62, 107, 148, 154, 204,
   236–38
   death of, 234
Lincoln, Mordecai, 47–48
Lincoln, Thomas ("Tad"),
   105–6, 160–61, 230
Lincoln, William Wallace
   ("Willie"), death of,
   106–8, 118, 148, 167
Lincoln, Nancy, 13, 19, 45–46,
   196
   death of, 46, 52, 164–66
Lincoln, Sarah, 59, 218
"The Long Nine," 42, 43
Louisville, Kentucky, 44, 50,
   158
Luther, Martin, 241
Lynn, Massachusetts, 151

McClellan, George B., 131, 141
McClernand, John A., 42
McMurtry, William, 42
Menard County, Illinois, 20, 23,
   38, 43, 49
Menter's Band, 113, 198
Meriden, Connecticut, 174
Mississippi River, 27, 71, 76
Mobile, Alabama, 29
Montauk, USS, 224

Moore, John, 42
Morris, Martin, Lincoln's letter
	to, 216–17

Nashville, Tennessee, 126
National Lincoln Monument,
	124
National Union League, 113
New Haven, Connecticut, 174
New Jersey Historical Society,
	134, 190
New Orleans, Lousiana, 24, 27,
	76–77, 136
New Salem, Illinois, 20, 22, 23,
	29, 31, 32, 38, 41, 48, 49,
	50, 163, 234
New York Lincoln Club, 167
Norwich, Connecticut, 173
Note Book of Reminiscences
	(Carter), 198

Old Capital Prison, 242
Our American Cousin, 185
Owen, Robert Dale, 115, 208

Parris, Illinois, 227
Petersburg, Illinois, 20, 32, 49
Philadelphia, Pennsylvania,
	175, 240
Pilgrim's Progress (Bunyan),
	19
Pope, John, 207
Portland, Maine, 90
Prince of Wales, 87–88
Princess Alexandria of
	Denmark, 87–88

Radford, Reuben, 163–64
Richardson, William A., 42
Richmond, capture of, 90, 208
Riney, Zacharia, 51
Rockport, Indiana, 194, 195
Rosecrans, William, 145–46
Rutledge, Ann, 20–22, 234–35

Sangamon River, 23, 51, 234
Savannah, Georgia, 29
Semple, James, 42
Seward, Frederick, 146
Seward, William, 13, 87, 146–47,
	155–56, 167–68, 192, 201,
	206, 238
	relationship with Lincoln,
	230–31
Shakespeare, William, 25
Shannon, Thomas, 60
Sherman, William T., 104, 147,
	203
Shields, James, 42, 61–63,
	71–72, 238
Shockle, Charles E., 204–6
Sizer, Nelson, 159
Smith, Caleb, 230
Smith, Franklin W., 140–41
South Starksboro, Vermont, 210
Speed, J. F., 44, 237
Spencer County, Indiana, *158*,
	194
Springfield, Illinois, 21, 23, 30,
	34, 44, 51, *54*, 59, 61, 70,
	76, 79, 80, 90, 155, 169,
	171, 179, 180, 212, 215,
	217, 234
Stanton, Edwin, 58, 101–4, 129,
	146, 148–50, 191–92, 196,
	204, 205, 231, 233, 238–46
	appointment as Secretary of
	War, 239–40
	appointment to Supreme
	Court, 244, 245
	conflict with Ulysses S.
	Grant, 244
	death of, 245
	place in history, 245–46
	tenders resignation, 152
Steedman, James B., 145–46
Stephens, Alexander, 155, 192
Stewart, Joseph B., 223–25
Stuart, John T., 41
Sumner, Charles, 243–44
Swett, Leonard, 209–10, 212

Taylor, Zachary, 52
Thomas, George H., 145, 146
Thomas, Lorenzo, 243
Thompson, Jacob, 90
Todd, Mary. *See* Lincoln, Mary
Todd, Robert S., 44, 236
Toombs, Robert, 239
Trenton, New Jersey, 20
Tyler, John, 116

Union Veteran Club, 212
Usher, John P., reminiscences
    of, 225–33

Vandalia, Illinois, 43
Vicksburg, fall of, 94
Victoria, Queen, 87–88

Wabash County, Illinois, 78
Wall Street, Lincoln's opinion
    of, 114–15
War Department, 88, 112, 129,
    131, 152, 153, 233

Washington, D.C., 29, 32, 51, 90,
    118, 134, 141, 148, 182,
    222, 223, 239
Watertown, New York, 109
Webster, Daniel, 89, 175
Weed, Thurlow, 167, 212
Welles, Gideon, 148, 204, 210,
    239
White House (Executive
    Mansion), 13, 92, 99, 100,
    105, 112, 113, 117, 121,
    129, 131, 144, 175, 177,
    206
White Pigeon Church, *96*
Whitman, Walt, account of
    Lincoln's assassination,
    184–88
Wilderness, battles of, 153
Williamsburg, battle of, 102
Wood, Ben, 232
Wood, Fernando, 232

Yale College, 174
Yates, Richard, 25, 34, 51, 213

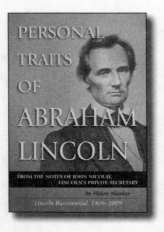

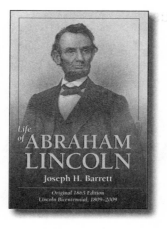

LINCOLN AND HIS WORLD

THE EARLY YEARS:
BIRTH TO ILLINOIS LEGISLATURE

Richard Lawrence Miller

Quoting from eyewitness accounts, Richard Lawrence
Miller allows Lincoln and his contemporaries to tell the
story of this monumental American and bring a fascinating
era of American history to life. The book covers Lincoln's
birth in 1809 through his first election to the Illinois
legislature in 1834.

$32.95 • Hardcover • 6 x 9 • 464 pages
0-8117-0187-5

WWW.STACKPOLEBOOKS.COM
1-800-732-3669